MW01012488

Math in Focus®

Singapore Math®
by Marshall Cavendish

Extra Practice and Homework

Program Consultant
Dr. Fong Ho Kheong

Authors
Chelvi Ramakrishnan
Michelle Choo

Marshall Cavendish
Education

U.S. Distributor

Houghton Mifflin Harcourt.
The Learning Company™

Grade **3A**

© 2020 Marshall Cavendish Education Pte Ltd

Published by Marshall Cavendish Education
Times Centre, 1 New Industrial Road, Singapore 536196
Customer Service Hotline: (65) 6213 9688
US Office Tel: (1-914) 332 8888 | Fax: (1-914) 332 8882
E-mail: cs@mceducation.com
Website: www.mceducation.com

Distributed by
Houghton Mifflin Harcourt
125 High Street
Boston, MA 02110
Tel: 617-351-5000
Website: www.hmhco.com/programs/math-in-focus

First published 2020

ISBN 978-0-358-10302-8

Printed in Singapore

3 4 5 6 7 8 9 10   1401   26 25 24 23 22
4500840209   B C D E F

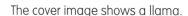

The cover image shows a llama.
Llamas live in herds on the mountains of South America.
A baby llama is called a cria.
Like horses and donkeys, llamas are often used to transport goods.
Llamas are intelligent animals and they can learn simple tasks or instructions quickly.
Their soft wool can be used to make warm clothes like scarves and sweaters.

Contents

Preface

Welcome!

Math in Focus® Extra Practice and Homework is written to be used with the **Math in Focus® Student Edition**, to support your learning.

This book provides activities and problems that closely follow what you have learned in the Student Edition.

- In **Activities**, you practice the concepts and skills you learned in the Student Edition, so that you can master the concepts and build your confidence.

- In **MATH JOURNAL**, you reflect on your thinking when you write down your thoughts about the math concepts you learned.

- In **PUT ON YOUR THINKING CAP!**, you develop your problem-solving and critical thinking skills, and challenge yourself to apply concepts in different ways.

This book also includes **SCHOOL-to-HOME CONNECTIONS**. Each family letter summarizes the learning objectives and the key mathematical vocabulary you are using. The letter also includes one or more activities that your family can do with you to support your learning further.

BLANK

SCHOOL-to-HOME
CONNECTIONS

Chapter 1

Numbers to 10,000

Dear Family,

In this chapter, your child will learn about numbers up to 10,000. Skills your child will practice include:

- counting, reading, and writing numbers up to 10,000
- stating the place and value of each digit in a 4-digit number
- comparing and ordering numbers to 10,000
- identifying the missing number(s) in a number pattern
- rounding numbers to the nearest ten and hundred

Math Practice

There are numerous real-life opportunities for your child to use and make sense of numbers up to 10,000. At the end of this chapter, you may want to carry out these activities with your child. These activities will help to strengthen your child's number sense.

Activity 1

- Draw a large place-value chart and place some beans, buttons, or game counters on it to represent a 4-digit number.
- Have your child write the number that is formed.
  An example is shown.

Number	Thousands	Hundreds	Tens	Ones
4,201	○ ○ ○ ○	○ ○		○

- Have your child talk about the place value of each digit in the chart. For example, the digit 4 in 4,201 stands for 4 thousands or 4,000.
- Make three 4-digit numbers and order them from greatest to least.

Math Talk

Help your child identify the **digits** in the number 2,478 and their **place value**. The digits are 2, 4, 7, and 8.

2,478

Thousands	Hundreds	Tens	Ones
2,	4	7	8

The digit 2 is in the thousands place. It stands for 2,000.
The digit 4 is in the hundreds place. It stands for 400.
The digit 7 is in the tens place. It stands for 70.
The digit 8 is in the ones place. It stands for 8.

Ask questions to help your child compare and order numbers, using **less than**, **greater than**, **least**, and **greatest**.
2,478   1,038   5,490

Which is greater, 2,478 or 5,490?
5,490 is greater than 2,478.

Which is less, 2,478 or 1,038?
1,038 is less than 2,478.

The numbers arranged from the least to the greatest are:
1,038   2,478   5,490
least   greatest

Activity 2

- Take your child to an electronic superstore to look at a variety of high-cost items. Or, look at electronic items and appliances advertised in flyers or online.
- Have your child pick out three appliances with prices in the thousands but below $10,000 and read each price aloud, pointing to each digit as he or she reads.
- Ask your child to compare the prices and order them from greatest to least or least to greatest.
- Select one of the items your child chose. Ask your child: "If I have a coupon for $10 off the cost, how much will I pay for this item? If I have a coupon for $100 off the cost, how much will I pay? If I have a coupon for $1,000 off the cost, how much will I pay?"
- Use the other items your child chose to repeat the activity.

Extra Practice and Homework
Numbers to 10,000

Activity 1   Counting to 10,000

Count to find each answer.

1

1,000

1,100   1,200   _____

_____   1,320   _____   1,340   _____

2
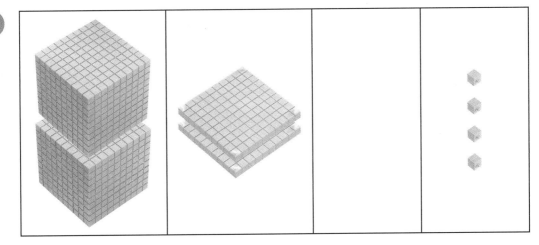

1,000   _____

_____   2,200

2,201   _____   2,203   _____

3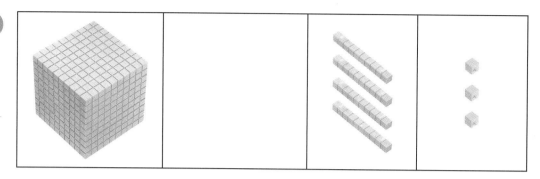

_____

1,010 _____ _____ 1,040

1,041 1,042 _____

4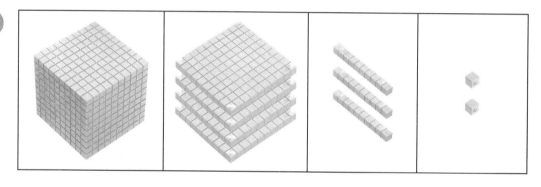

_____

1,100 _____ _____ 1,400

_____ 1,420 _____

1,431 _____

Find each missing number.
Count on by ones, tens, hundreds, or thousands.

5 82 1,082 2,082 _____ _____ _____

6 4,105 4,205 4,305 _____ _____ _____

7 3,047 3,057 3,067 _____ _____ _____

8 6,895 6,896 6,897 _____ _____ _____

Chapter 1
Extra Practice and Homework
Numbers to 10,000

Activity 2 Place Value

Fill in each blank.

1

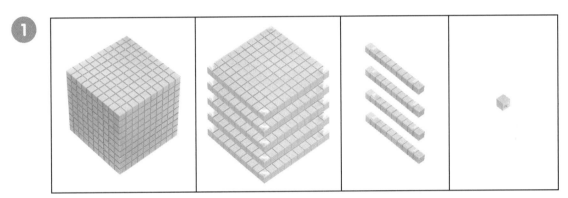

$1,000 + 500 + 40 + 1 =$ _____

$1,000$, 500, 40, and 1 make _____.

2

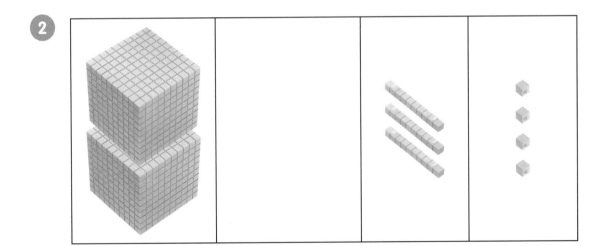

$2,000 + 30 + 4 =$ _____

$2,000$, 30, and 4 make _____.

3 a   7,000 + 5 = _____

    b   6,000 + 100 + 7 = _____

    c   _____ + 900 + 4 = 8,904

    d   9,000 + _____ + 4 = 9,074

    e   7,856 = 7,000 + _____ + 50 + 6

    f   3,432 = 3,000 + _____ + 30 + 2

Compare both sides of the sentence. Then, find the value of the missing digit.

What is the value of each ☺?

4 a   9,621 = ☺ + 621   b   7,000 + ☺ + 49 = 7,549

       ☺ = _____   ☺ = _____

Find each missing number.

5 a

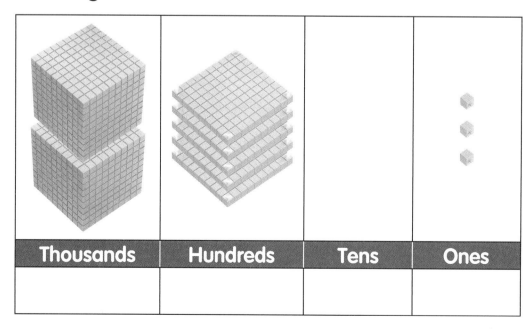

Thousands	Hundreds	Tens	Ones

b The digit _____ is in the thousands place. ← 2, 5 0 3

The digit _____ is in the hundreds place. ←

The digit _____ is in the tens place. ←

The digit _____ is in the ones place. ←

c The value of the digit 2 is _____.

The value of the digit 5 is _____.

The value of the digit 0 is _____.

The value of the digit 3 is _____.

6 a

Thousands	Hundreds	Tens	Ones

b The digit _____ is in the thousands place. ← 4, 2 3 5

The digit _____ is in the hundreds place. ←

The digit _____ is in the tens place. ←

The digit _____ is in the ones place. ←

c The value of the digit 4 is _____.

The value of the digit 2 is _____.

The value of the digit 3 is _____.

The value of the digit 5 is _____.

7 In 5,426

a the value of the digit 5 is _____. ← 5, 4 2 6

b the value of the digit 4 is _____. ←

c the value of the digit 2 is _____. ←

d the value of the digit 6 is _____. ←

8 In 4,703

    a   the value of the digit 4 is _____. ← 4, 7 0 3

    b   the value of the digit 7 is _____. ←

    c   the value of the digit 0 is _____. ←

    d   the value of the digit 3 is _____. ←

9 In 9,854

    a   the value of the digit 9 is _____. ← 9, 8 5 4

    b   the value of the digit 8 is _____. ←

    c   the value of the digit 5 is _____. ←

    d   the value of the digit 4 is _____. ←

Use a place-value chart to help you find the place and the value of each digit.

10 **a**   In 7,019, the digit _____ is in the thousands place.

    b   In 7,019, the digit _____ is in the hundreds place.

    c   In 7,019, the digit _____ is in the tens place.

    d   In 7,019, the digit _____ is in the ones place.

⑪ a   In 2,548, the value of the digit 4 is _____.

b   In 3,467, the value of the digit 3 is _____.

c   In 6,321, the value of the digit 1 is _____.

d   In 8,675, the value of the digit 7 is _____.

Write each number in expanded form, standard form, and word form.

⑫ 2,000
   800
   30

Expanded form: _____

Standard form: _____

Word form: _____

⑬ 8,000
   200
   5

Expanded form: _____

Standard form: _____

Word form: _____

Expanded form: _____

Standard form: _____

Word form: _____

Expanded form: _____

Standard form: _____

Word form: _____

Expanded form: _____

Standard form: _____

Word form: _____

17

Expanded form: _____

Standard form: _____

Word form: _____

Fill in each blank.

18 Write a 4-digit number that has the digit 5 in the thousands

place and the digit 1 in the tens place. _____

19 Write a number that has the digit 8 in the thousands place but

is less than 8,050. _____

20 ☺ + 2 = 3,002

☺ + 725 = _____

6,000 + ☺ + 20 + 6 = _____

Chapter

1

Extra Practice and Homework
Numbers to 10,000

Activity 3 Comparing and Ordering Numbers

Fill in each blank.

1 **a** Which is greater, 1,233 or 1,241?

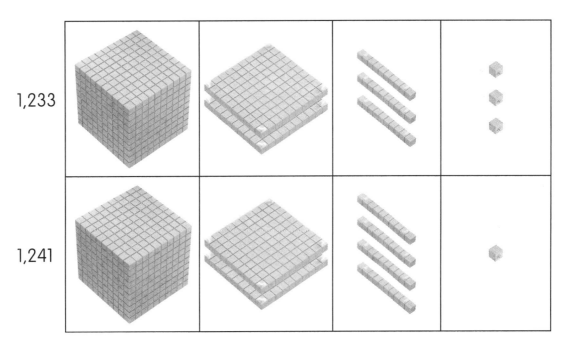

1,233

1,241

_____ is greater than _____.

b Which is less, 1,120 or 1,234?

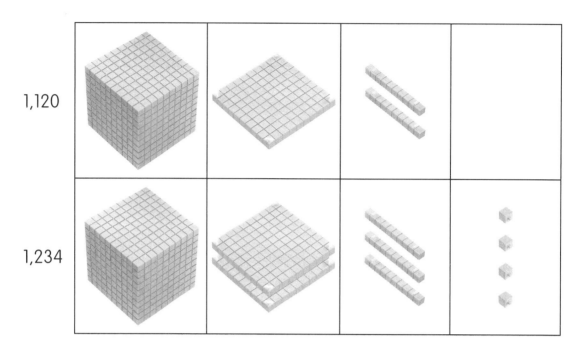

_____ is less than _____.

2 **a** Which is less, 3,409 or 710?

Thousands	Hundreds	Tens	Ones
3	4	0	9
	7	1	0

_____ is less than _____.

b Which is greater, 6,820 or 5,946?

Thousands	Hundreds	Tens	Ones
6	8	2	0
5	9	4	6

_____ is greater than _____.

c Which is greater, 9,238 or 9,328?

Thousands	Hundreds	Tens	Ones
9	2	3	8
9	3	2	8

_____ is greater than _____.

d Which is less, 2,785 or 2,759?

Thousands	Hundreds	Tens	Ones
2	7	8	5
2	7	5	9

_____ is less than _____.

Compare each pair of numbers. Write > or <.

3 a 1,387 $\bigcirc$ 1,385

b 3,628 $\bigcirc$ 3,682

Fill in each blank with "greater than" or "less than."

4 a 1,999 is _____ 2,000.

b 2,391 is _____ 2,099.

5 Order the numbers from greatest to least.

greatest   least

6 Order the numbers from least to greatest.

least   greatest

Look at the number lines and fill in each blank.

7 **a** Which is greater, 3,800 or 2,600?

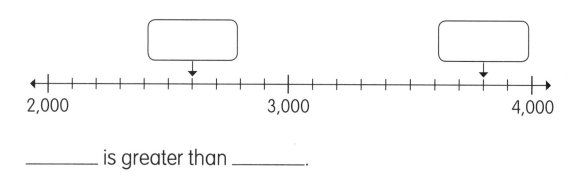

_____ is greater than _____.

b Which is less, 5,120 or 5,150?

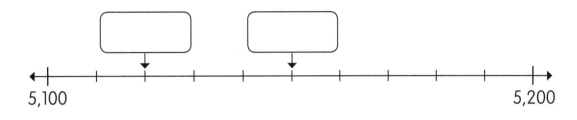

_____ is less than _____.

c Which is greater, 3,861 or 3,853?

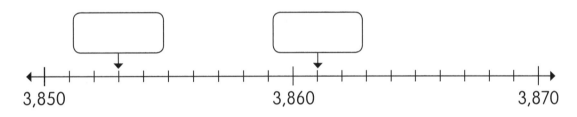

_____ is greater than _____.

Look for a pattern. Then, fill in each blank.

8

9

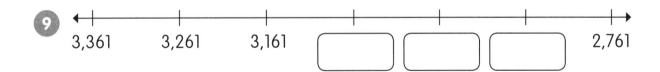

10

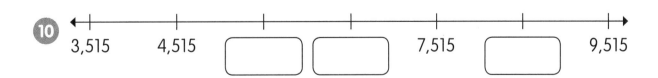

11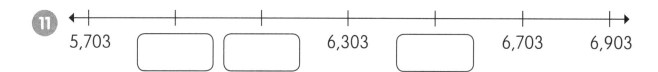

5,703 [ ] [ ] 6,303 [ ] 6,703 6,903

12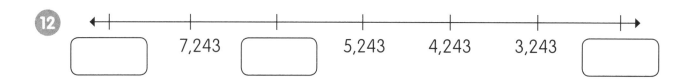

[ ] 7,243 [ ] 5,243 4,243 3,243 [ ]

13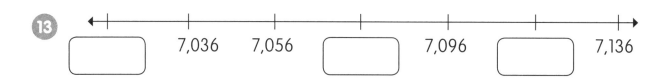

[ ] 7,036 7,056 [ ] 7,096 [ ] 7,136

Complete each number pattern. Draw a number line to help you.

14

_____ _____ _____ 5,755 5,765 5,775

15

8,625 8,725 _____ _____ 9,025 9,125

16

862 1,862 _____ 3,862 4,862 _____

17

6,315 6,215 6,115 _____ _____ _____

Solve.

18 Using the digits 6, 4, 7, and 0 only once, make a number greater than 7,300.

Chapter
1

Extra Practice and Homework
Numbers to 10,000

Activity 4 Rounding Numbers to the Nearest Ten

Fill in each place-value chart. Then, fill in each blank with "less than," "or greater," "do not change," "add 1 to," or "zero."

1 Round 1,034 to the nearest ten.

Thousands	Hundreds	Tens	Ones

The digit to the right of the tens place is _____ 5.

So, _____ the digit in the tens place.

Then, replace the digit to the right of the tens place with _____.

1,034 is _____ when rounded to the nearest ten.

2 Round 2,547 to the nearest ten.

Thousands	Hundreds	Tens	Ones

The digit to the right of the tens place is 5 _____.

So, _____ the digit in the tens place.

Then, replace the digit to the right of the tens place with _____.

2,547 is _____ when rounded to the nearest ten.

Mark (X) each number on the number line.
Then, round each number to the nearest ten.

3 Round 6,721 to the nearest ten.

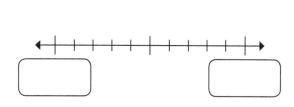

6,721 is between _____ and _____.

6,721 is nearer to _____ than to _____.

6,721 is _____ when rounded to the nearest ten.

4 Round 9,285 to the nearest ten.

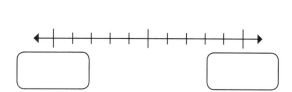

9,285 is exactly halfway between _____ and _____.

9,285 is _____ when rounded to the nearest ten.

Round the price of each item to the nearest ten dollars.

Item	Price	Rounded to the Nearest Ten Dollars
5 Book	$45	
6 Carpet	$213	
7 Sofa set	$4,599	

Solve.

8 What is the least number that gives 1,680 when rounded to the nearest ten?

Extra Practice and Homework
Numbers to 10,000

Activity 5 Rounding Numbers to the Nearest Hundred

Fill in each place-value chart. Then, fill in each blank with "less than," "or greater," "do not change," "add 1 to," or "zero(s)."

1 Round 950 to the nearest hundred.

Hundreds	Tens	Ones

The digit to the right of the hundreds place is 5 _____.

So, _____ the digit in the hundreds place.

Then, replace the digit to the right of the hundreds place

with _____.

950 is _____ when rounded to the nearest hundred.

2 Round 1,234 to the nearest hundred.

Thousands	Hundreds	Tens	Ones

The digit to the right of the hundreds place is _____ 5.

So, _____ the digit in the hundreds place.

Then, replace the digit to the right of the hundreds place

with _____.

1,234 is _____ when rounded to the nearest hundred.

Mark (X) each number on the number line.
Then, round each number to the nearest hundred.

3 Round 6,750 to the nearest hundred.

6,750 is exactly halfway between
_____ and _____.

6,750 is _____ when rounded
to the nearest hundred.

4 Round 7,996 to the nearest hundred.

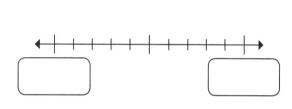

7,996 is between _____
and _____.

7,996 is nearer to _____
than to _____.

7,996 is _____ when
rounded to the nearest hundred.

Round each number to the nearest hundred.

	Number	Rounded to the Nearest Hundred
5	47	
6	755	
7	1,345	

Solve.

8 What is the greatest number that gives 6,000 when rounded to
the nearest hundred?

1 **Mathematical Habit 7** **Make use of structure**

Look at the numbers below.

(6,128)   (6,228)

a   Write three sentences showing how they are similar.

_____

_____

_____

b   Write a sentence showing how they are different.

_____

_____

2 Look at the numbers below.

(4,816)   (3,814)

a   Write two sentences showing how they are similar.

_____

_____

b   Write two sentences showing how they are different.

_____

_____

_____

1 | Mathematical Habit **7** Make use of structure

The numbers are arranged in a pattern.
Fill in the missing numbers.

1,042	1,041		1,039	
				1,039
				1,040
	1,048	1,047		
		1,046		
	1,046		1,044	1,043

2 | Mathematical Habit **2** Use mathematical reasoning

I am a 4-digit number.
The digits in my tens and ones places are the same.
The digit in my hundreds place is 4 more than the digit in my tens place.
The digit in the thousands place is 1 less than the digit in my hundreds place.

Thousands	Hundreds	Tens	Ones

I am _____.

There are many possible answers.

SCHOOL-to-HOME
CONNECTIONS

Addition Within 10,000

Dear Family,

In this chapter, your child will learn how to add numbers within 10,000. Skills your child will practice include:
- identifying arithmetic patterns
- adding 2-digit numbers mentally
- adding fluently within 1,000
- adding up to 4-digit numbers without regrouping
- adding up to 4-digit numbers with regrouping
- solving real-world problems

Math Practice

There are numerous real-life opportunities for your child to add numbers. At the end of this chapter, you may want to carry out these activities with your child. These activities will help your child practice adding numbers.

Activity 1

- Go online to find actual numbers to add, being sure that the total, or sum, does not exceed 10,000.
- Ask your child to guess how many people visit a favorite place such as a local park, sports field, or museum on a particular weekend.
- Then have your child find the total number of visitors on a particular weekend.

Activity 2

- Go online to find the cost of admission for adults and children to your favorite movie theater.
- Have your child round each cost to the nearest dollar.
- Then, have your child mentally add the cost of going to see a movie together.

Math Talk

Explain to your child that a **sum** is the total, or answer to an addition problem. Ask your child to find the sum of 1,536 and 2,442.

$1,536 + 2,442 = 3,978$
3,978 is the sum of 1,536 and 2,442.

Discuss **regrouping** with your child. For example, regroup:
10 ones into 1 ten;
10 tens into 1 hundred; and
10 hundreds into 1 thousand.

Help your child regroup to find the sum of 1,536 and 2,875.

```
   ¹ ¹ ¹
   1, 5 3 6
 + 2, 8 7 5
 ───────────
   4, 4 1 1
```

Regroup 11 ones into 1 ten 1 one.
Regroup 11 tens into 1 hundred 1 ten.
Regroup 14 hundreds into 1 thousand 4 hundreds.
$1,536 + 2,875 = 4,411$

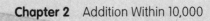

BLANK

Chapter 2

Extra Practice and Homework
Addition Within 10,000

Activity 1 Addition Patterns

Add each pair of numbers by making 10.

1 6 + 7 = _____

2 4 + 9 = _____

3 9 + 6 = _____

4 8 + 8 = _____

Add each pair of numbers by making 5.

5 9 + 5 = _____

6 6 + 5 = _____

7 5 + 8 = _____

8 5 + 7 = _____

Add each set of numbers.

9 4 + 3 + 8 = _____

10 9 + 5 + 7 = _____

11 7 + 8 + 2 = _____

12 6 + 4 + 5 = _____

Complete each sum in two different ways.

13 ? + 3 + ? = 9

_____ + 3 + _____ = 9

_____ + 3 + _____ = 9

14 ? + ? + 7 = 15

_____ + _____ + 7 = 15

_____ + _____ + 7 = 15

© 2020 Marshall Cavendish Education Pte Ltd

Describe each pattern. Use the addition table to help you.

15 Look at the diagonal of 5s. What do you notice?

_____

_____

16 Add the two diagonals across any square in the addition table. What do you notice?

_____

_____

17 Add the numbers in the diagonals shown. What do you notice about the sums?

+	0	1	2	3	4	5	6	7	8	9
0	0	1	2	3	4	5	6	7	8	9
1	1	2	3	4	5	6	7	8	9	10
2	2	3	4	5	6	7	8	9	10	11
3	3	4	5	6	7	8	9	10	11	12
4	4	5	6	7	8	9	10	11	12	13
5	5	6	7	8	9	10	11	12	13	14
6	6	7	8	9	10	11	12	13	14	15
7	7	8	9	10	11	12	13	14	15	16
8	8	9	10	11	12	13	14	15	16	17
9	9	10	11	12	13	14	15	16	17	18

_____

_____

Chapter 2
Extra Practice and Homework
Addition Within 10,000

Activity 2 Mental Addition

Add each pair of numbers mentally. Use the number bonds to help you.

① Find the sum of 73 and 25.

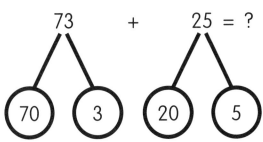

Can you add 73 and 25 in another way?

 Add the tens.

70 + 20 = _____

 Add the ones.

3 + 5 = _____

73 + 25 = _____ + _____

= _____

The sum of 73 and 25 is _____.

② Find the sum of 24 and 55.

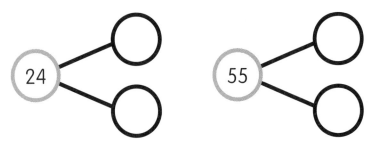

The sum of 24 and 55 is _____.

3 Find the sum of 22 and 64.

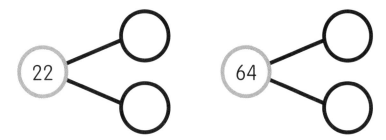

The sum of 22 and 64 is _____.

4 Add 76 and 23.

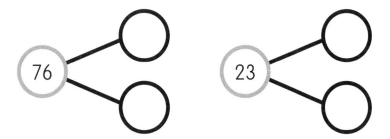

$76 + 23 =$ _____

Add each pair of numbers mentally. Draw number bonds to help you.

5 $16 + 81 =$ _____   **6** $48 + 31 =$ _____

© 2020 Marshall Cavendish Education Pte Ltd

Add each pair of numbers mentally. Use the number bond to help you.

7 Find the sum of 36 and 47.

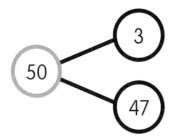

> Can you add 36 and 47 in another way?

STEP 1 Add 50 to 36.

36 + 50 = _____

STEP 2 Subtract 3 from the result.

_____ − 3 = _____

The sum of 36 and 47 is _____.

8 Find the sum of 37 and 45.

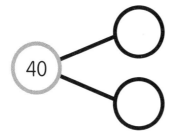

The sum of 37 and 45 is _____.

9 Add 46 and 34.

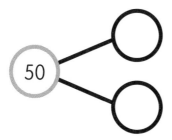

46 + 34 = _____

10 41 + 59 = _____

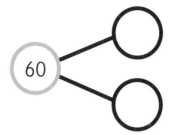

11 24 + 38 = _____

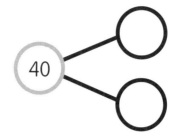

12 15 + 47 = _____

13 46 + 48 = _____

14 Find the sum of 19 and 98.

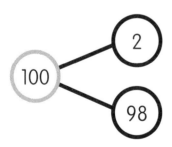

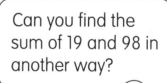
Can you find the sum of 19 and 98 in another way?

STEP 1 Add 100 to 19.

19 + 100 = _____

STEP 2 Subtract 2 from the result.

_____ – 2 = _____

The sum of 19 and 98 is _____.

Extra Practice and Homework Grade 3A

15 Find the sum of 26 and 96.

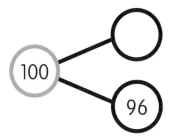

The sum of 26 and 96 is _____.

16 Find the sum of 38 and 95.

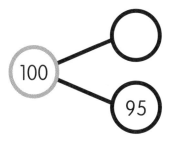

The sum of 38 and 95 is _____.

17 Add 92 and 39.

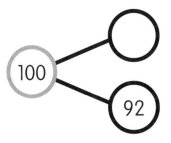

$92 + 39 =$ _____

Add each pair of numbers mentally. Draw number bonds to help you.

18 $42 + 99 =$ _____

19 $76 + 98 =$ _____

Solve. Show your work.

20 Explain how you would add 5 and 98.

21 Explain how you would find the sum of 76 and 48.

Extra Practice and Homework
Addition Within 10,000

Activity 3   Adding Fluently Within 1,000

Add. Show your work.

1 137 + 52 = _____

2 267 + 312 = _____

3 361 + 314 = _____

4 789 + 210 = _____

5 What is the sum of 346 and 242?

_____

6 260 is added to 721. What is the result?

_____

7 $457 + 92 =$ _____

8 $199 + 88 =$ _____

9 $539 + 86 =$ _____

10 $164 + 364 =$ _____

11 $283 + 562 =$ _____

12 $376 + 291 =$ _____

13 521 + 187 = _____

14 715 + 193 = _____

15 285 + 137 = _____

16 637 + 268 = _____

17 696 + 158 = _____

18 737 + 179 = _____

Circle the tag with the number that is 1 more than the number on Ashley's tag.

Ashley
629

19 725 + 142
= _____

20 378 + 256
= _____

21 264 + 598
= _____

22 254 + 376
= _____

23 452 + 124
= _____

24 647 + 285
= _____

Activity 4 Adding Without Regrouping

Fill in each blank.

1 Find the sum of 1,344 and 112.

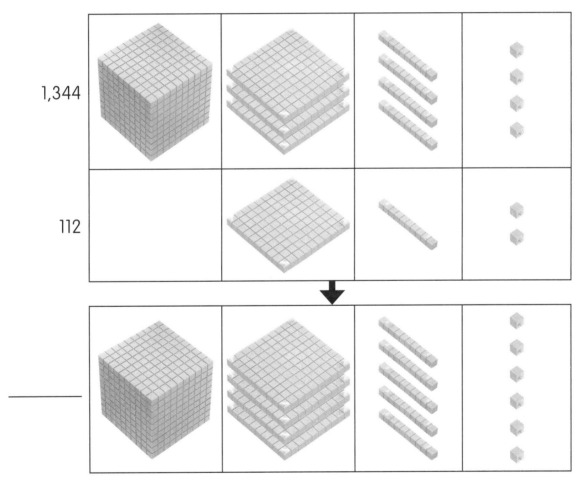

1,344

112

$$\begin{array}{r} 1,\ 3\ 4\ 4 \\ +\quad 1\ 1\ 2 \\ \hline \end{array}$$

The sum of 1,344 and 112 is _____.

2 Add 2,410 and 1,023.

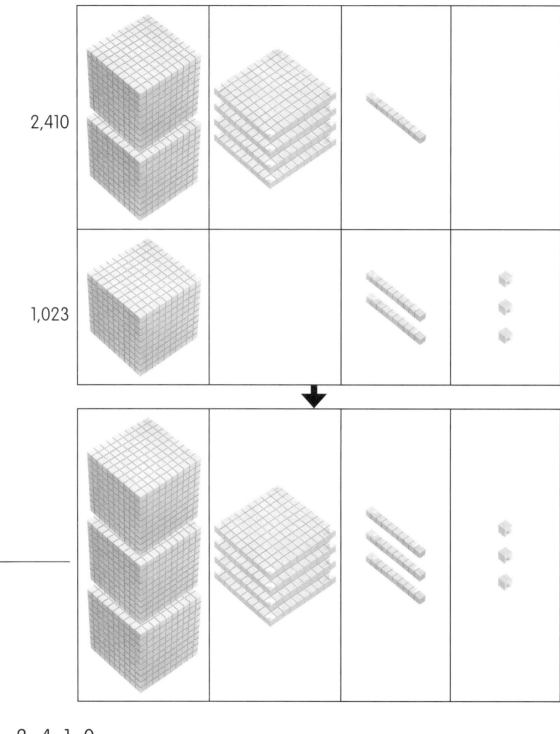

$$\begin{array}{r} 2,4\ 1\ 0 \\ +\ 1,0\ 2\ 3 \\ \hline \end{array}$$

2,410 + 1,023 = _____

3 Find the sum of 1,854 and 12.

1,854 + 12 = _____

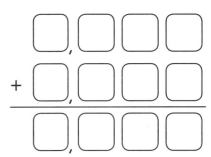

4 Find the sum of 5,362 and 506.

5,362 + 506 = _____

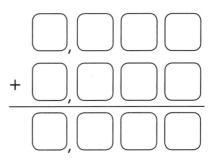

5 Find the sum of 6,542 and 3,050.

6,542 + 3,050 = _____

Add.

6
```
  5, 4 1 3
+       8 2
```

7
```
  6, 2 1 0
+     7 6 5
```

8
```
  5, 3 2 4
+     3 5 1
```

9
```
  3, 0 2 5
+     8 5 4
```

10
```
  6, 7 1 3
+     2 8 0
```

11
```
  3, 4 3 0
+ 1 0 4 8
```

12
```
  3, 1 5 7
+ 2, 2 4 2
```

13
```
  5, 5 6 6
+ 4, 2 1 1
```

Add. Show your work in each space provided. Then, check if your answers are reasonable.

14 3,360 + 29

15 2,070 + 20

16 2,020 + 73

17 2,516 + 423

18 9,060 + 300

19 2,468 + 500

20 2,500 + 273

21 4,376 + 3,000

22 7,462 + 2,537

Fill in each blank.

23

```
    2, ☐ 4 3
  +     3 1 ☐
  ─────────────
    ☐, 8 5 5
```

24

```
    6, 1 7 ☐
  +     6 ☐ 9
  ─────────────
    6, ☐ 8 9
```

Chapter 2

Extra Practice and Homework
Addition Within 10,000

Activity 5   Adding with Regrouping

Fill in each blank.

1 Add 1,500 and 500.

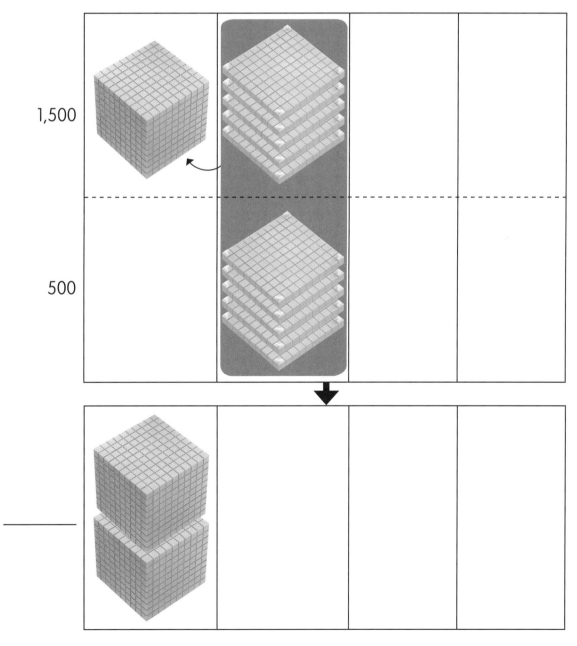

$$\begin{array}{r} 1,500 \\ +500 \\ \hline \end{array}$$

$$\boxed{}$$

$1,500 + 500 =$ _____

Add.

2
$$\begin{array}{r} 5,600 \\ +1,700 \\ \hline \end{array}$$
$$\boxed{}$$

3
$$\begin{array}{r} 6,800 \\ +1,200 \\ \hline \end{array}$$
$$\boxed{}$$

4
$$\begin{array}{r} 7,145 \\ +924 \\ \hline \end{array}$$
$$\boxed{}$$

5
$$\begin{array}{r} 4,812 \\ +2,374 \\ \hline \end{array}$$
$$\boxed{}$$

Add. Show your work in each space provided. Then, check if your answers are reasonable.

6 $5,823 + 454 =$ _____

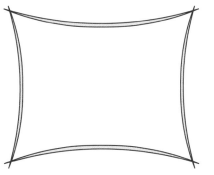

7 $6,651 + 518 =$ _____

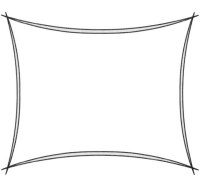

8 $3,253 + 4,804 =$ _____

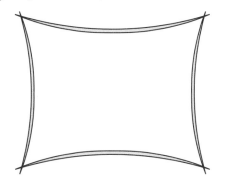

9 $6,512 + 2,745 =$ _____

Fill in each blank.

10 Add 2,845 and 1,356.

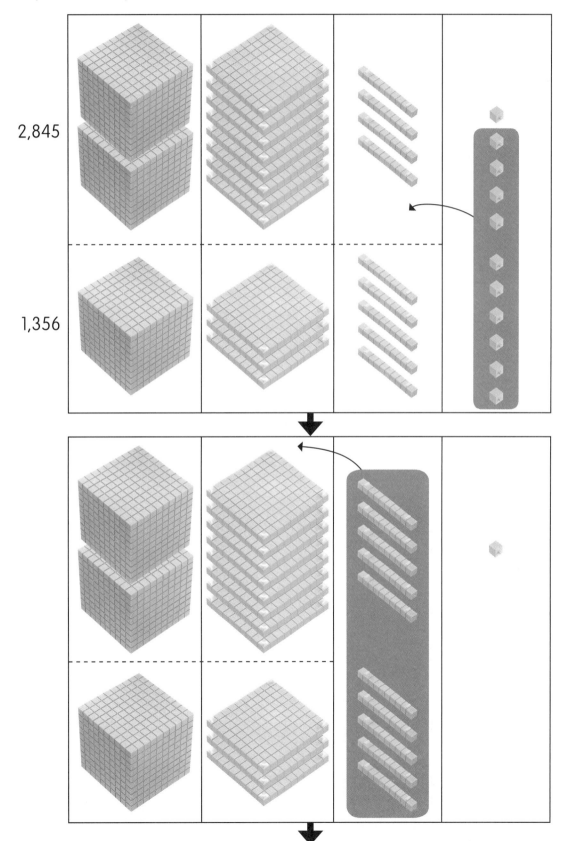

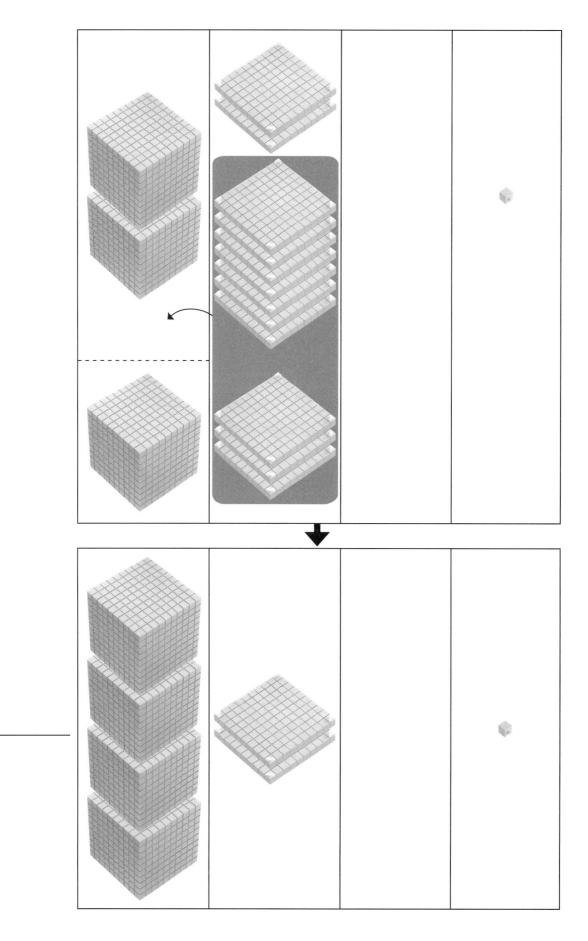

$$\begin{array}{r} 2,8\ 4\ 5 \\ +\ 1,3\ 5\ 6 \\ \hline \end{array}$$

2,845 + 1,356 = _____

Add.

11
$$\begin{array}{r} 2,9\ 8\ 7 \\ +\quad\ 5\ 8 \\ \hline \end{array}$$

12
$$\begin{array}{r} 3,9\ 1\ 4 \\ +\quad\ 8\ 6 \\ \hline \end{array}$$

13
$$\begin{array}{r} 4,9\ 9\ 8 \\ +\quad\ 7\ 6 \\ \hline \end{array}$$

14
$$\begin{array}{r} 5,9\ 8\ 7 \\ +\quad\ 9\ 5 \\ \hline \end{array}$$

15
$$\begin{array}{r} 2,8\ 9\ 7 \\ +\quad\ 9\ 2\ 8 \\ \hline \end{array}$$

16
$$\begin{array}{r} 3,7\ 9\ 6 \\ +\quad\ 2\ 1\ 5 \\ \hline \end{array}$$

17
$$\begin{array}{r} 6,9\ 4\ 3 \\ +\quad\ 6\ 5\ 7 \\ \hline \end{array}$$

18
$$\begin{array}{r} 1,2\ 6\ 6 \\ +\quad\ 7\ 5\ 4 \\ \hline \end{array}$$

19
$$\begin{array}{r} 3,6\ 2\ 2 \\ +\ 1,7\ 9\ 8 \\ \hline \end{array}$$

20
$$\begin{array}{r} 3,4\ 2\ 9 \\ +\ 1,5\ 9\ 7 \\ \hline \end{array}$$

21
$$\begin{array}{r} 3,6\ 7\ 4 \\ +\ 1,6\ 6\ 7 \\ \hline \end{array}$$

22
$$\begin{array}{r} 6,4\ 3\ 5 \\ +\ 2,6\ 8\ 9 \\ \hline \end{array}$$

Add. Show your work in each space provided. Then, check if your answers are reasonable.

23 26 + 1,984 = _____

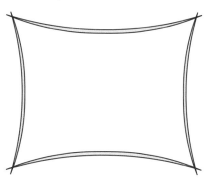

24 6,956 + 98 = _____

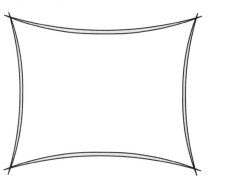

25 561 + 6,789 = _____

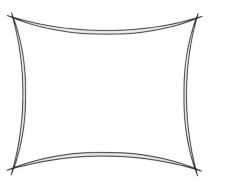

26 7,938 + 165 = _____

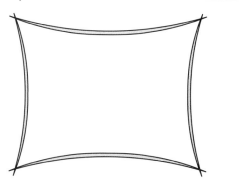

27 3,046 + 2,975 = _____

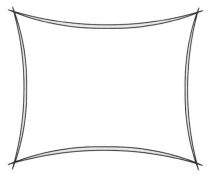

28 4,266 + 1,769 = _____

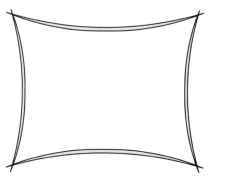

Fill in each blank.

29
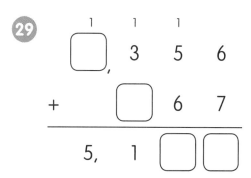

```
      1   1   1
   [ ] , 3   5   6
 +     [ ]   6   7
 ─────────────────
   5 ,  1  [ ] [ ]
```

30
```
      1   1   1
   6 , [ ] [ ] [ ]
 +         7   4   5
 ─────────────────
   7 ,  0   0   0
```

Chapter 2

Extra Practice and Homework
Addition Within 10,000

Activity 6 Real-World Problems: Addition

**Solve. Show your work. Use the bar model to help you.
Then, check if your answers are reasonable.**

1 Hana walked 1,350 steps to reach Point A, another 2,396 steps
to reach Point B, and another 3,147 steps to reach Point C. How
many steps did she take in all to reach Point C?

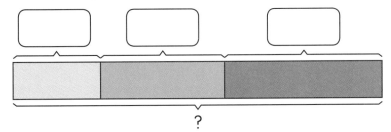

_____ ◯ _____ = _____

She took _____ steps to reach
Point B.

_____ ◯ _____ = _____

She took _____ steps in all to
reach Point C.

 STEP 1 Understand the
problem.

 STEP 2 Think of a plan.

 STEP 3 Carry out the plan.

 STEP 4 Check the answer.

2 A biking team raises $4,250 for charity.
A running team raises $825 more than the biking team.

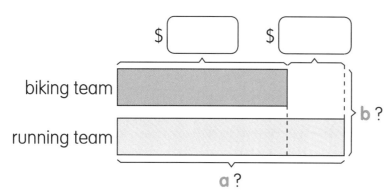

$ [____] $ [____]

biking team

running team

b ?

a ?

a How much money does the running team raise?

$_____ ◯ $_____ = $_____

The running team raises $_____.

b How much money do both teams raise in all?

$_____ ◯ $_____ = $_____

Both teams raise $_____ in all.

Solve. Show your work. Draw bar models to help you.
Then, check if your answers are reasonable.

3️⃣ A middle school has 3,756 students. It has 455 fewer students than an elementary school.

    a How many students does the elementary school have?

    b How many students do both schools have in all?

4 There are 5,740 visitors at Exhibition A.
There are 2,871 visitors at Exhibition B.
Another 1,388 visitors arrive at Exhibition B.

    a   How many visitors are there at Exhibition B now?

    b   How many visitors are there in all at the two exhibitions?

5 A shop sold 2,390 bottles of water on Saturday.
   350 more bottles were sold on Sunday than on Saturday.

   a   How many bottles of water were sold on Sunday?

   b   How many bottles of water were sold over the weekend?

6 Jade had 1,458 paper clips.
She had 396 fewer paper clips than Pedro.

    a   How many paper clips did Pedro have?

    b   How many paper clips did they have in all?

7 A packet of magnets costs $9.97.
A key chain costs $3.57 more than the packet of magnets.
How much money do the two items cost in all?

8 A hair clip costs $2.50.
A pair of gloves costs $9.87.
Mr. Young has a total of $15.75 to buy these two items.

   a   How much do the hair clip and the pair of gloves cost in all?

   b   How much money will Mr. Young have left?

1 Mathematical Habit **7** **Make use of structure**

What 4-digit number can you add to 3,467 to get a 4-digit even number? Explain how you can get the answer.

2 Mathematical Habit **7** **Make use of structure**

What 4-digit number can you add to 3,467 to get a 4-digit odd number? Explain how you can get the answer.

Mathematical Habit 1 Persevere in solving problems

Find the missing number. How did you get your answer?

```
        1      1      1
    2,  8   [    ]  6
+   4,  4   4    [    ]
  ─────────────────────
    7,  [    ]  0    4
```

SCHOOL-to-HOME
CONNECTIONS

Subtraction Within 10,000

Dear Family,

In this chapter, your child will learn to subtract numbers within 10,000. Skills your child will practice include:
- subtracting 2-digit numbers mentally
- subtracting fluently within 1,000
- subtracting without regrouping
- subtracting with regrouping
- solving real-world problems

Math Practice

There are numerous real-life opportunities for your child to subtract numbers. At the end of this chapter, you may want to carry out these activities with your child. These activities will help your child practice subtracting numbers.

Activity 1

- Go online to find the total number of participants in a marathon or a charity event, such as a charity walk or bike ride.
- Find out how many adults and children took part. Ensure that the number of adults and children are each within 10,000.
- Then, have your child calculate the difference between the two.

Activity 2

- Ask your child to identify a favorite local entertainment venue, such as a bowling alley, a video arcade, or a movie theater.
- Go online to find the price of a ticket for an adult and a child.
- Round each price to the nearest dollar. Then, ask your child to mentally subtract to find the difference between the two.

 **Math Talk**

Help your child understand that **difference** is the answer to a subtraction problem. Ask your child to find the difference between 3,695 and 1,243.
$3{,}695 - 1{,}243 = 2{,}452$
2,452 is the difference between 3,695 and 1,243.

Discuss **regrouping** with your child. For example, regroup:
1 ten into 10 ones;
1 hundred into 10 tens; and
1 thousand into 10 hundreds.

Help your child regroup to find the difference between 6,210 and 4,635.

$$\begin{array}{r} \overset{5}{\cancel{6}}\,,\overset{11}{\cancel{2}}\,\overset{10}{\cancel{1}}\,\overset{10}{\cancel{0}} \\ -\ 4{,}6\,3\,5 \\ \hline 1{,}5\,7\,5 \end{array}$$

Regroup 1 ten into 0 tens 10 ones.
Regroup 2 hundreds into 1 hundred 10 tens.
Regroup 6 thousands into 5 thousands 10 hundreds.
$6{,}210 - 4{,}635 = 1{,}575$

BLANK

Chapter 3
Extra Practice and Homework
Subtraction Within 10,000

Activity 1   Mental Subtraction

Subtract each pair of numbers mentally.
Use the number bonds to help you.

1 Find the difference between 78 and 63.

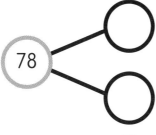

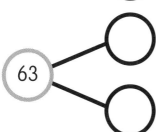

Is there another way to find the difference between 78 and 63?

 Subtract the tens.

70 − 60 = _____

 Subtract the ones.

8 − 3 = _____

78 − 63 = _____ + _____

= _____

The difference between 78 and 63 is _____.

2 Find the difference between 89 and 57.

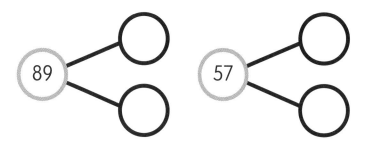

The difference between 89 and 57 is _____.

3 Subtract 33 from 75.

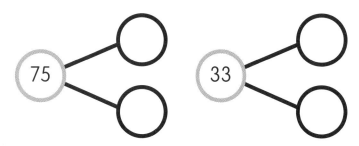

75 − 33 = _____

**Subtract each pair of numbers mentally.
Draw number bonds to help you.**

4 84 − 23 = _____

5 55 − 31 = _____

Subtract each pair of numbers mentally. Use the number bond to help you.

6 Find the difference between 83 and 47.

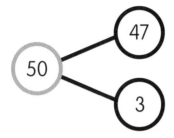

Is there another way to find the difference between 83 and 47?

 Subtract 50 from 83.

$83 - 50 =$ _____

 Add 3 to the result.

_____ $+ 3 =$ _____

The difference between 83 and 47 is _____.

7 Find the difference between 92 and 35.

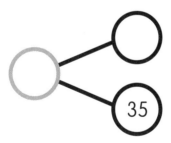

The difference between 92 and 35 is _____.

8 Subtract 22 from 91.

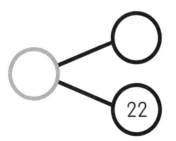

$91 - 22 =$ _____

9 43 − 14 = _____

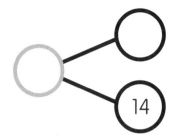

10 84 − 38 = _____

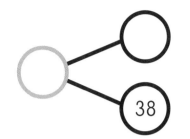

Subtract each pair of numbers mentally.
Draw number bonds to help you.

11 68 − 29 = _____

12 90 − 45 = _____

Solve. Show your work.

13 Explain how you would subtract 36 from 98.

14 Explain how you would find the difference between 56 and 37.

Chapter 3
Extra Practice and Homework
Subtraction Within 10,000

Activity 2   Subtracting Fluently Within 1,000

Subtract. Then, circle the book that the boys are reading.

(373)

1 $875 - 32 =$ _____

2 $698 - 257 =$ _____

3 $587 - 214 =$ _____

4 $859 - 821 =$ _____

5 $968 - 317 =$ _____

6 $375 - 150 =$ _____

Subtract. Show your work in each space provided.

7 185 – 96 = _____

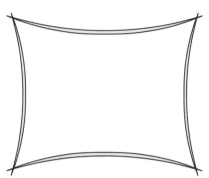

8 816 – 77 = _____

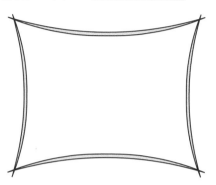

9 215 – 169 = _____

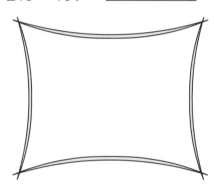

10 314 – 186 = _____

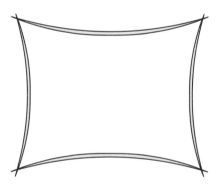

11 440 – 95 = _____

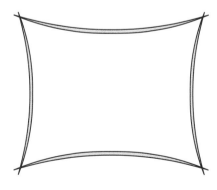

12 505 – 368 = _____

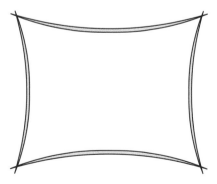

Extra Practice and Homework Grade 3A

13 630 − 245 = _____

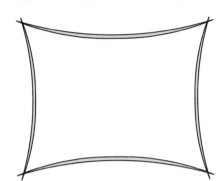

14 727 − 199 = _____

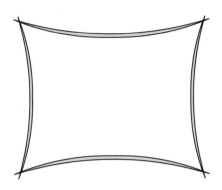

15 753 − 495 = _____

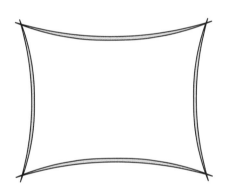

16 920 − 287 = _____

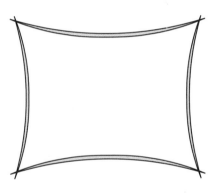

17 931 − 489 = _____

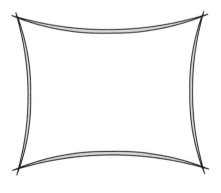

18 500 − 248 = _____

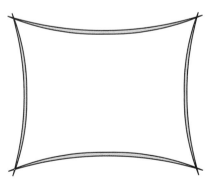

Subtract and match.

19 842 – 315 = _____ •

                                     •
215

20 734 – 519 = _____ •

                                     •
306

21 831 – 87 = _____ •

                                     •
377

22 716 – 609 = _____ •

                                     •
744

23 Find the difference between •

692 and 315. _____

                                     •
527

24 Find the difference between •

276 and 582. _____

                                     •
107

Chapter 3
Extra Practice and Homework
Subtraction Within 10,000

Activity 3 Subtracting Without Regrouping

Fill in each blank.

1 Subtract 234 from 2,354.

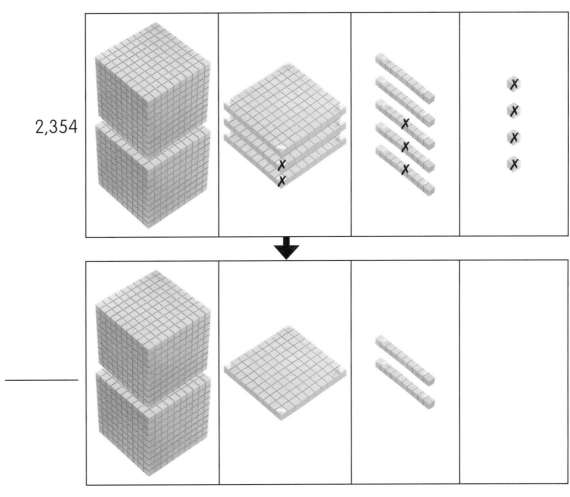

2,354

$$\begin{array}{r} 2{,}3\ 5\ 4 \\ -\ \ \ 2\ 3\ 4 \\ \hline \end{array}$$

2,354 − 234 = _____

2️⃣ Find the difference between 3,635 and 2,201.

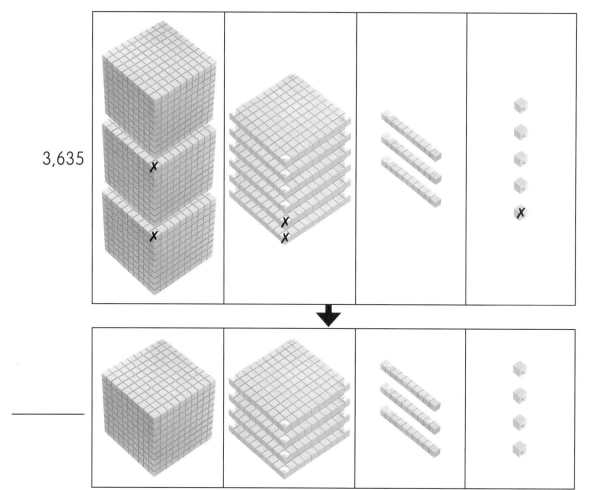

3,635

```
   3, 6 3 5
 - 2, 2 0 1
 ┌─────────┐
 │         │
 └─────────┘
```

3,635 − 2,201 = _____

The difference between 3,635 and 2,201 is _____.

3️⃣ Subtract 138 from 9,349.

```
   9, 3 4 9
 -    1 3 8
 ┌─────────┐
 │         │
 └─────────┘
```

9,349 − 138 = _____

Extra Practice and Homework Grade 3A

4 Find the difference between 4,321 and 7,352.

```
    7, 3 5 2
 -  4, 3 2 1
```

The difference between 4,321 and 7,352 is _____.

Subtract.

5
```
   5, 5 6 4
 -       2 3
```

6
```
   8, 9 7 5
 -       6 4
```

7
```
   3, 8 1 9
 -     7 0 5
```

8
```
   9, 6 4 6
 -     5 2 3
```

9
```
   6, 4 8 1
 -     3 5 0
```

10
```
   3, 6 0 6
 - 2, 5 0 3
```

11
```
   5, 2 8 6
 - 5, 1 2 3
```

12
```
   7, 2 4 9
 - 6, 2 3 8
```

13
```
   9, 7 8 5
 - 7, 5 4 1
```

Subtract. Show your work in each space provided. Then, check if your answers are reasonable.

14 9,786 − 72 = _____

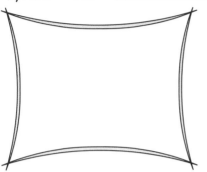

15 6,593 − 81 = _____

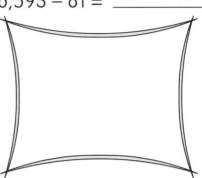

16 8,421 − 310 = _____

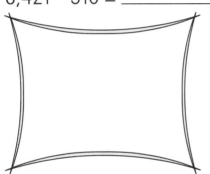

17 4,875 − 164 = _____

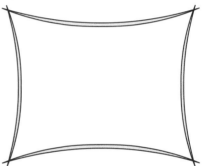

18 7,493 − 4,342 = _____

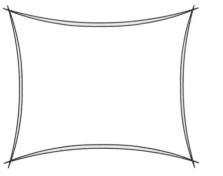

19 5,847 − 2,615 = _____

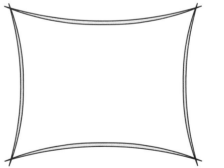

Fill in each blank.

20

```
    3, ☐ 9  7
  − 2, 3  9 ☐
  ──────────
    ☐, 1  0  6
```

21

```
    ☐, 0  7 ☐
  − 1, ☐  1  3
  ──────────
    5, 0  6  1
```

Activity 4 Subtracting with Regrouping

Fill in each blank.

1 Subtract 753 from 2,910.

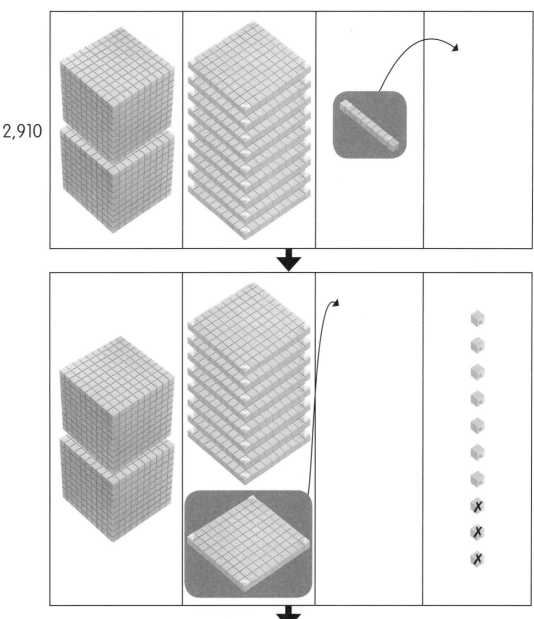

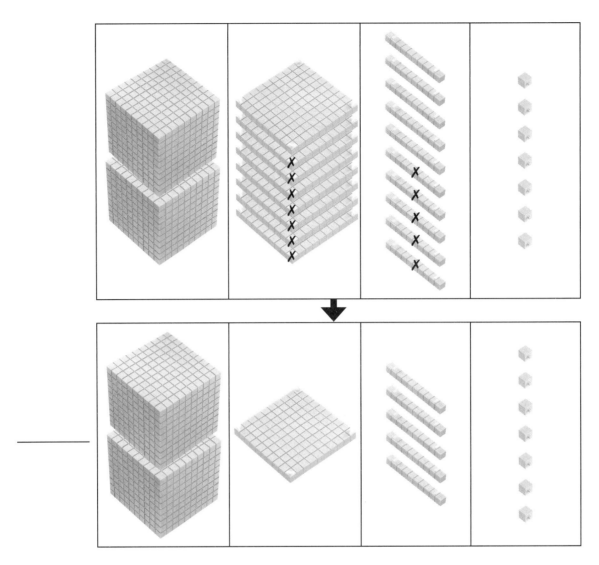

$$\begin{array}{r} 2,910 \\ -753 \\ \hline \end{array}$$

$\boxed{}$

2,910 − 753 = _____

2 Find the difference between 2,236 and 4,312.

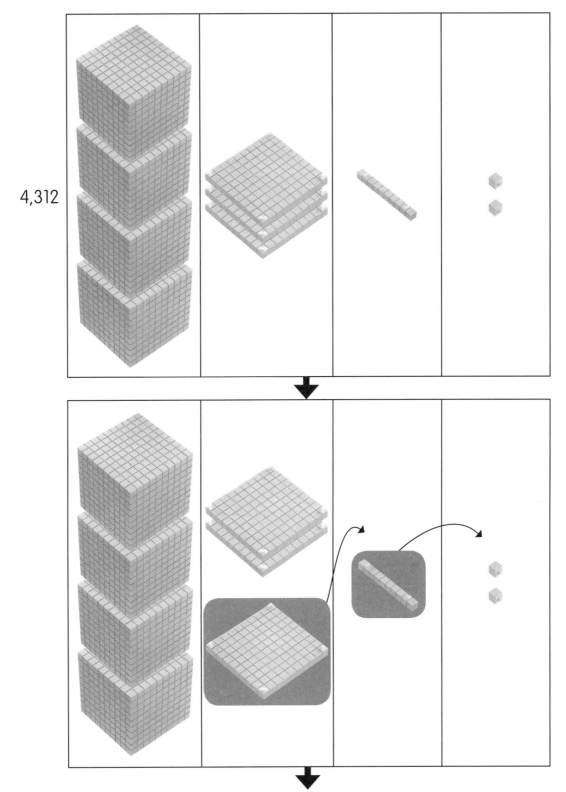

4,312

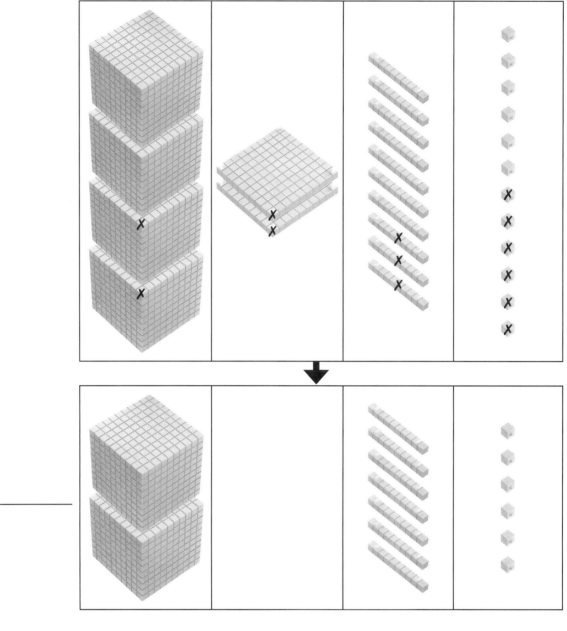

$$\begin{array}{r} 4,\ 3\ 1\ 2 \\ -\ 2,\ 2\ 3\ 6 \\ \hline \end{array}$$

4,312 − 2,236 = _____

The difference between 4,312 and 2,236 is _____.

Subtract.

3
```
   2, 9 4 3
 −      5 9
```

4
```
   6, 5 7 0
 −      9 1
```

5
```
   3, 6 1 3
 −    2 7 4
```

6
```
   6, 5 2 4
 −    1 3 8
```

7
```
   5, 7 3 2
 − 4, 0 6 4
```

8
```
   9, 6 2 5
 − 3, 2 8 8
```

Subtract. Show your work in each space provided. Then, check if your answers are reasonable.

9 7,824 − 489 = _____

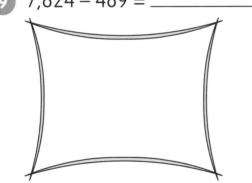

10 2,655 − 1,397 = _____

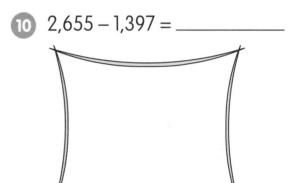

Fill in each blank.

11
```
          5   10   12
   8,  [  ]   X̶    2̶
 − 3,     1  [  ]   5
 ───────────────────
   5,     4    3    7
```

12
```
        7    13   11
 [  ],  8̶   [  ]   X̶
 − 7,   [  ]   5    6
 ───────────────────
   2,    4    8    5
```

Subtract. Then, find out what the message at the bottom of the page is.

13

$8{,}542 - 383 = \boxed{}$ _ _ _ $2{,}652 - 597 = \boxed{}$. _

$5{,}626 - 248 = \boxed{}$ . . . $4{,}861 - 1{,}089 = \boxed{}$.

$9{,}512 - 5{,}363 = \boxed{}$ . . . . $3{,}731 - 1{,}255 = \boxed{}$. _ . .

Morse Code								
A	B	C	D	E	F	G	H	I
· _	_ · · ·	_ · _ ·	_ · ·	·	· · _ ·	_ _ ·	· · · ·	· ·
J	K	L	M	N	O	P	Q	R
· _ _ _	_ · _	· _ · ·	_ _	_ ·	_ _ _	· _ _ ·	_ _ · _	· _ ·
S	T	U	V	W	X	Y	Z	
· · ·	_	· · _	· · · _	· _ _	_ · · _	_ · _ _	_ _ · ·	

Each answer is represented by a symbol in the Morse code.

Match the letters of the Morse code to the answers below.

"_____ _____ _____ _____ _____!"

   4,149   3,772   2,476   2,476   8,159

Fill in each blank.

14 Subtract 1,987 from 2,110.

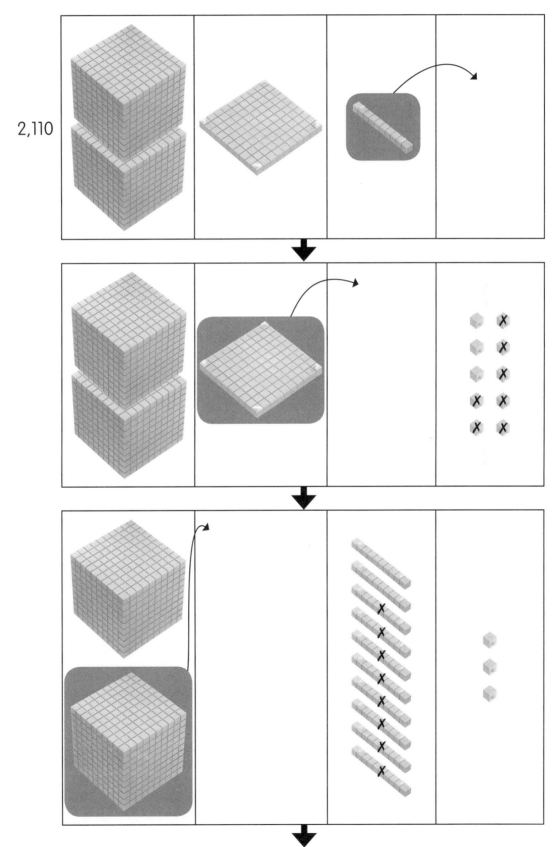

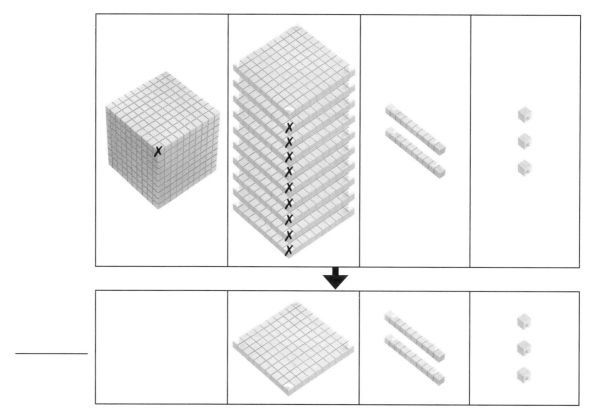

$$
\begin{array}{r}
2,1\ 1\ 0 \\
-\ 1,9\ 8\ 7 \\
\hline
\end{array}
$$

2,110 – 1,987 = _____

Regroup and subtract.

15
$$
\begin{array}{r}
1,4\ 3\ 6 \\
-\ \ \ 6\ 8\ 8 \\
\hline
\end{array}
$$

16
$$
\begin{array}{r}
2,1\ 1\ 1 \\
-\ \ \ 1\ 9\ 7 \\
\hline
\end{array}
$$

17

$$\begin{array}{r} 6,345 \\ -\ \ \ 469 \\ \hline \end{array}$$

18

$$\begin{array}{r} 7,556 \\ -\ 3,589 \\ \hline \end{array}$$

19

$$\begin{array}{r} 4,873 \\ -\ 1,984 \\ \hline \end{array}$$

20

$$\begin{array}{r} 5,160 \\ -\ 3,217 \\ \hline \end{array}$$

21

$$\begin{array}{r} 9,191 \\ -\ 2,563 \\ \hline \end{array}$$

22

$$\begin{array}{r} 8,956 \\ -\ 4,987 \\ \hline \end{array}$$

Color the answers from questions **15** to **22** to find the path to the present.

4,987	3,876	1,864
5,533	1,914	6,628
1,235	748	9,713
6,753	2,889	276
1,943	3,969	438
3,967	5,876	1,176	5,763

Start

Regroup and subtract.

23 6,717 − 1,725 = [   ]

24 7,342 − 2,502 = [   ]

25 7,965 − 978 = [   ]

26 8,513 − 566 = [   ]

27 2,152 − 1,648 = [   ]

28 3,287 − 1,779 = [   ]

29 4,124 − 1,858 = [   ]

30 5,213 − 2,796 = [   ]

31 7,654 − 2,875 = [   ]

32 9,133 − 7,269 = [   ]

Regroup and subtract. Then, color the spaces that contain the answers to identify an endangered animal* in Southeast Asia.

33
$$\begin{array}{r} 8,214 \\ -635 \\ \hline \end{array}$$

34
$$\begin{array}{r} 8,462 \\ -999 \\ \hline \end{array}$$

35
$$\begin{array}{r} 3,287 \\ -1,779 \\ \hline \end{array}$$

36
$$\begin{array}{r} 6,522 \\ -5,783 \\ \hline \end{array}$$

37
$$\begin{array}{r} 3,150 \\ -1,274 \\ \hline \end{array}$$

38
$$\begin{array}{r} 9,731 \\ -8,875 \\ \hline \end{array}$$

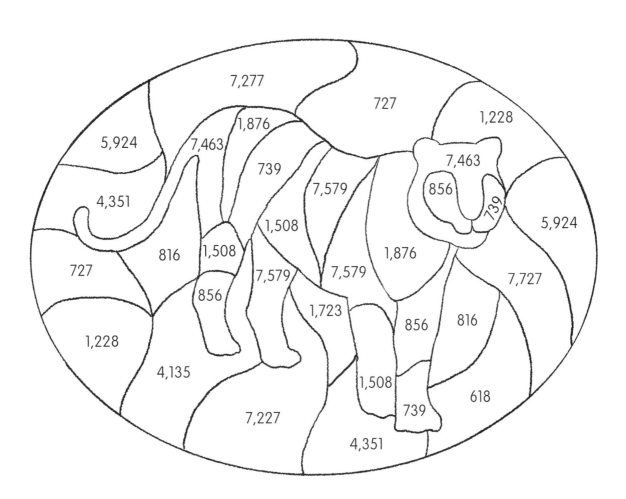

*An animal is endangered when there are so few of its kind left that it could become extinct.

Fill in each blank.

39 Find the difference between 3,652 and 1,821. _____

40 Find the difference between 3,610 and 8,231. _____

41 The difference between 6,117 and 725 is _____.

42 The difference between 4,327 and 9,084 is _____.

43 There are two numbers.
The greater number is 2,731.
The greater number is 842 more than the lesser number.

What is the lesser number? _____

44 There are two numbers.
The greater number is 3,839.
The difference between the two numbers is 1,398.

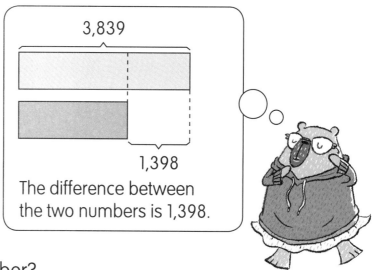

3,839

1,398
The difference between
the two numbers is 1,398.

What is the lesser number? _____

45 $6{,}525 - \underline{\hspace{2cm}} = 6{,}125$

46 $1{,}593 - \underline{\hspace{2cm}} = 93$

47 $7{,}403 = 7{,}003 + \underline{\hspace{2cm}}$

48 $\underline{\hspace{2cm}} - 60 = 1{,}700$

49 $2{,}170 = \underline{\hspace{2cm}} + 300$

50 $\underline{\hspace{2cm}} + 500 = 3{,}580$

Fill in each blank.

51 Subtract 1,777 from 2,000.

2,000

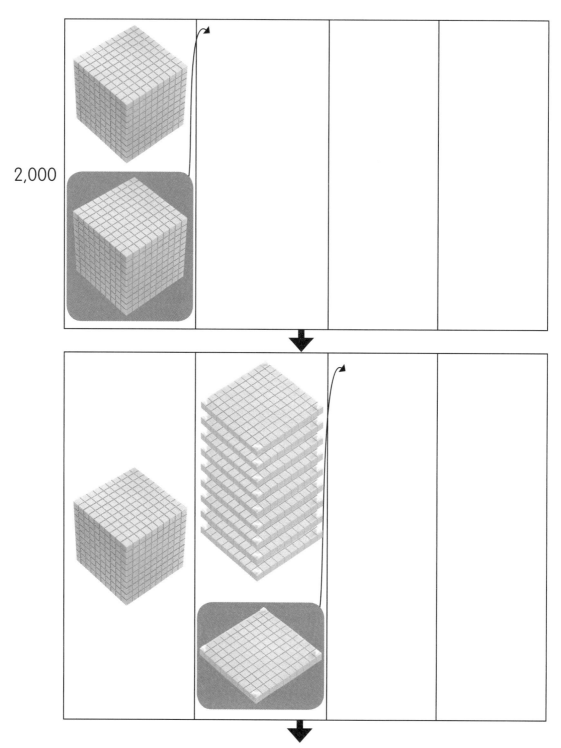

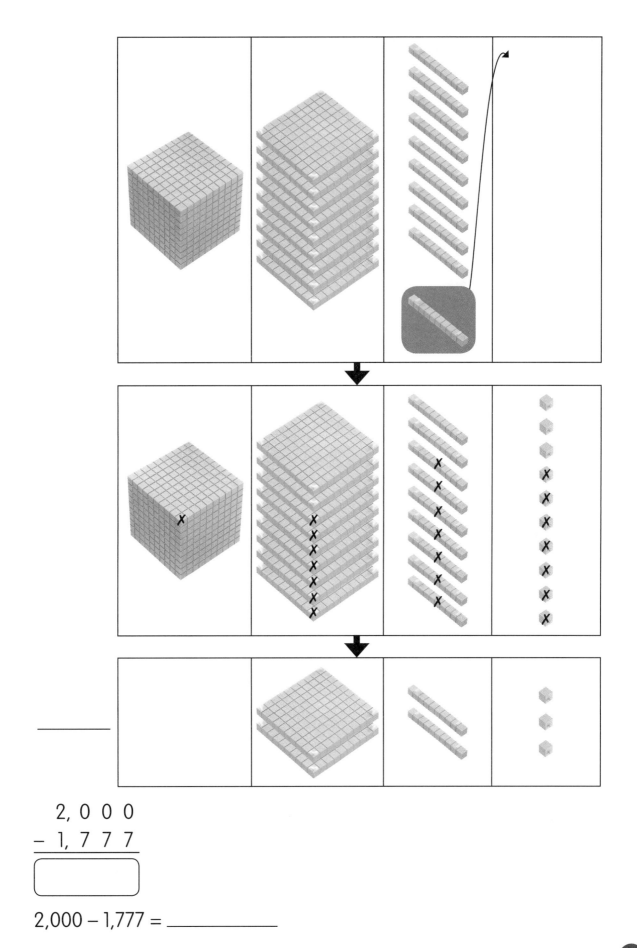

$$\begin{array}{r} 2,000 \\ -\ 1,777 \\ \hline \end{array}$$

2,000 – 1,777 = _____

Subtract. Then, check if your answers are reasonable.

52
$$\begin{array}{r} 2{,}060 \\ -\quad 78 \\ \hline \end{array}$$

53
$$\begin{array}{r} 3{,}000 \\ -\quad 29 \\ \hline \end{array}$$

54
$$\begin{array}{r} 1{,}060 \\ -\quad 343 \\ \hline \end{array}$$

55
$$\begin{array}{r} 5{,}000 \\ -\quad 764 \\ \hline \end{array}$$

56
$$\begin{array}{r} 2{,}006 \\ -\quad 358 \\ \hline \end{array}$$

57
$$\begin{array}{r} 6{,}003 \\ -1{,}437 \\ \hline \end{array}$$

58
$$\begin{array}{r} 3{,}006 \\ -2{,}515 \\ \hline \end{array}$$

59
$$\begin{array}{r} 8{,}004 \\ -5{,}476 \\ \hline \end{array}$$

Fill in each blank.

60
$$\begin{array}{r} \cancel{4}{,}\ \cancel{0}\ \cancel{0}\ 11 \\ -\ \square{,}\ 5\ \square\ 7 \\ \hline 3{,}\ 4\ 4\ 4 \end{array}$$

61
$$\begin{array}{r} \cancel{7}{,}\ \cancel{0}\ \cancel{0}\ \cancel{0} \\ -\ 1{,}\ \square\ \square\ \square \\ \hline 5{,}\ 0\ 0\ 1 \end{array}$$

Extra Practice and Homework
Subtraction Within 10,000

Activity 5   Real-World Problems: Subtraction

**Solve. Show your work. Use the bar model(s) to help you.
Then, check if your answers are reasonable.**

1   Class A collects 9,876 bottles for a recycling program.
Class B collects 1,234 fewer bottles than Class A.
Class C collects 2,345 fewer bottles than Class B.
How many bottles does Class C collect?

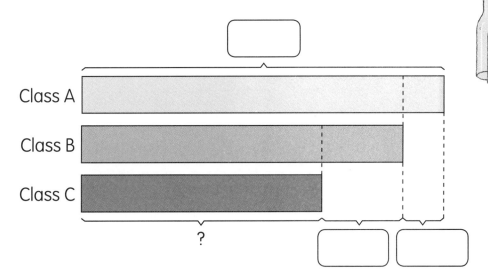

_____ ◯ _____ = _____

Class B collects _____ bottles.

_____ ◯ _____ = _____

Class C collects _____ bottles.

2 Ms. Smith had $5,098. A trip to Iceland cost $2,455.
A trip to Paris cost $696 less than the trip to Iceland.
She paid for both trips.

    a How much did the trip to Paris cost?

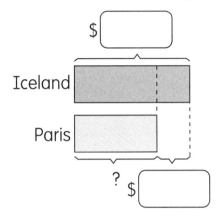

$ _____ \bigcirc $ _____ = $ _____

The trip to Paris cost $_____.

    b How much money did Ms. Smith pay for both trips?

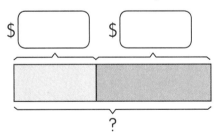

$ _____ \bigcirc $ _____ = $ _____

Ms. Smith paid $_____ for both trips.

Solve. Show your work. Draw bar models to help you.
Then, check if your answers are reasonable.

3 Emma and Ryan have 2,693 cards in all.
Emma has 1,568 cards.
Jacob has 372 fewer cards than Ryan.
How many cards does Jacob have?

4 A bookstore has 4,320 books and magazines.
It has 2,169 books. The rest are magazines.

a   How many magazines does the bookstore have?

b   There are 1,493 fashion magazines.
The rest are sports magazines.
How many sports magazines does the bookstore have?

5 Anya's rope is 1,831 centimeters long.
Jack's rope is 379 centimeters shorter than Anya's rope.

  a   How long is Jack's rope?

  b   Jack uses 645 centimeters of his rope.
       How long is his remaining rope?

6 A school sets aside $4,756 for its sports fund.
It sets aside $1,297 less for its library fund.

    a   How much money is in the library fund?

    b $948 is spent from the library fund.
           How much money is left in the library fund?

7 A farm harvested 5,461 potatoes and 2,539 apples.
The workers packed 3,850 potatoes and apples into boxes.

  a How many potatoes and apples did the farm harvest
  in all?

  b How many potatoes and apples were left unpacked?

8 Mr. Wilson pays $26.49 for his meal.
It is $11.52 more expensive than Ms. Hill's meal.
Ms. Mendoza's meal is $2.22 cheaper than Ms. Hill's meal.
How much does Ms. Mendoza's meal cost?

Name: _____ Date: _____

1 **Mathematical Habit 2** **Use mathematical reasoning**

What 4-digit number can you subtract from 5,406 to get a 4-digit odd number? Explain how you can get the answer.

2 **Mathematical Habit 2** **Use mathematical reasoning**

What 4-digit number can you subtract from 5,406 to get a 4-digit even number? Explain how you can get the answer.

Mathematical Habit 7 Make use of structure

The difference between two numbers is 100.
The lesser number is between 90 and 100.
List all the possible pairs of numbers.

Lesser Number	Greater Number	Difference

SCHOOL-to-HOME
CONNECTIONS

Chapter 4

Multiplication Tables

Dear Family,

In this chapter, your child will learn about the multiplication tables of 6, 7, 8, 9, 11, and 12, and how multiplication and division are related. Skills your child will practice include:

- skip counting by 6, 7, 8, 9, 11, and 12
- learning the multiplication tables of 6, 7, 8, 9, 11, and 12
- using multiplication facts to derive division facts
- identifying multiplication patterns

Math Practice

There are numerous real-life opportunities for your child to use multiplication and division facts. At the end of this chapter, you may want to carry out these activities with your child. These activities will help to reinforce your child's understanding of the facts.

Activity 1

- First, decide on a multiplication table, for example, 6. Then, start counting from 1. Take turns to say the next number in the series.
- At each product, replace it by saying "Up!" instead. For example, 1, 2, 3, 4, 5, *Up!*, 7, 8, 9, 10, 11, *Up!*, 13, 14, 15, 16, 17, *Up!*, …
- When your child is proficient with the multiplication table of 6, repeat the activity using the multiplication tables of 7, 8, 9, 11, or 12.

Activity 2

- Have your child roll a number cube to get a number, for example, 3.
- Then, have your child use the number to write a multiplication fact of 7, for example, 3 × 7 = 21.
- Repeat the activity several times, using multiplication facts of 8, 9, 11, or 12.

 Math Talk

Explain to your child that an **array model** is an arrangement in rows and columns. For example,

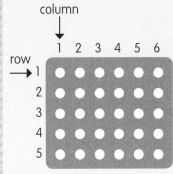

$5 \times 6 = 30$

Help your child understand the **area model** of multiplication. For example,

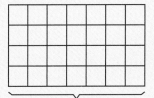

$4 \times 7 = 28$

Ask your child to explain how **multiplication facts** and **division facts** are related. That is, how does knowing a multiplication fact help him or her find a related division fact?

Prompt the discussion by using an example. If $5 \times 7 = 35$ and $7 \times 5 = 35$, then we know that $35 \div 5 = 7$ and $35 \div 7 = 5$.

Write two related multiplication facts and have your child find the related division facts.

© 2020 Marshall Cavendish Education Pte Ltd

BLANK

Extra Practice and Homework
Multiplication Tables

Activity 1   Multiplying by 6

Find and circle the multiplication facts of 6 in the puzzle.
The multiplication facts (without operation signs) can be vertical, horizontal, or diagonal.
An example has been done for you.

 1

81	39	45	23	8	91	67	48
15	2	42	10	9	74	6	55
33	6	32	6	50	8	44	80
70	12	54	60	7	60	2	1
5	3	24	6	4	3	6	95
11	6	7	36	6	6	12	10
4	18	30	6	36	18	28	40
24	6	4	9	42	1	6	6

Multiply. Use multiplication facts you know to find other multiplication facts.

2   $6 \times 6 =$ _____

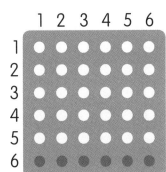

_____ $\times 6 =$ _____

_____ $\times 6 =$ _____

_____ $\times 6 =$ _____ $+$ _____

$=$ _____

3 8 × 6 = _____

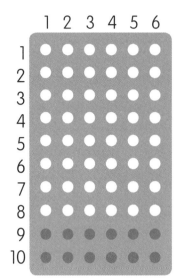

_____ × 6 = _____

_____ × 6 = _____

_____ × 6 = _____ − _____

= _____

4 7 × 6 = _____

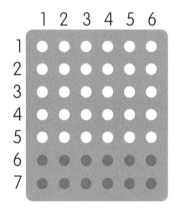

_____ × 6 = _____

_____ × 6 = _____

_____ × 6 = _____ + _____

= _____

5 9 × 6 = _____

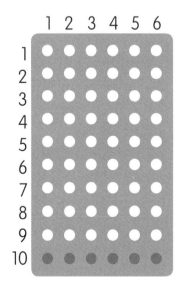

_____ × 6 = _____

_____ × 6 = _____

_____ × 6 = _____ − _____

= _____

Chapter 4

Extra Practice and Homework
Multiplication Tables

Activity 2 Multiplying by 7

Find and circle the multiplication facts of 7 in the puzzle.
The multiplication facts (without operation signs) can be vertical, horizontal, or diagonal.
An example has been done for you.

 1

56	10	6	29	49	3	61	77
7	35	7	52	7	4	7	28
8	7	1	70	7	56	2	47
75	5	22	7	83	58	7	39
63	14	68	14	7	2	15	8
7	26	3	5	54	20	92	42
9	7	80	7	13	49	7	7
21	0	60	35	8	51	90	6

Multiply. Use multiplication facts you know to find other multiplication facts.

2 $6 \times 7 = $ _____

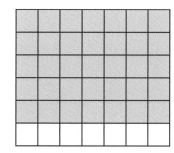

_____ $\times 7 = $ _____

_____ $\times 7 = $ _____

_____ $\times 7 = $ _____ + _____

= _____

3 8 × 7 = _____

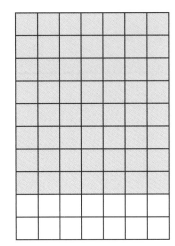

_____ × 7 = _____

_____ × 7 = _____

_____ × 7 = _____ – _____

= _____

4 9 × 7 = _____

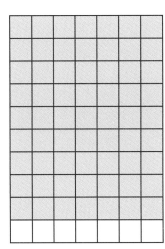

_____ × 7 = _____

_____ × 7 = _____

_____ × 7 = _____ – _____

= _____

5 7 × 7 = _____

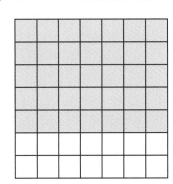

_____ × 7 = _____

_____ × 7 = _____

_____ × 7 = _____ + _____

= _____

Extra Practice and Homework Grade 3A

Extra Practice and Homework
Multiplication Tables

Activity 3 Multiplying by 8

Find and circle the multiplication facts of 8 in the puzzle.
The multiplication facts (without operation signs) can be vertical,
horizontal, or diagonal.
An example has been done for you.

1

2	16	3	72	2	6	16	8
10	8	8	8	6	8	24	8
24	8	16	9	7	48	4	72
8	64	40	8	72	8	9	56
9	5	56	4	32	5	8	40
8	10	8	80	8	40	72	1
72	8	7	40	4	64	48	80
64	80	56	70	32	48	30	70

**Multiply. Use multiplication facts you know to find other
multiplication facts.**

2 $7 \times 8 =$ _____

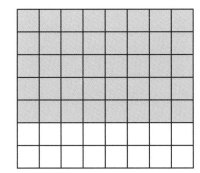

_____ $\times\, 8 =$ _____

_____ $\times\, 8 =$ _____

_____ $\times\, 8 =$ _____ $+$ _____

$=$ _____

3 $6 \times 8 =$ _____

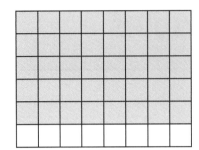

_____ $\times 8 =$ _____

_____ $\times 8 =$ _____

_____ $\times 8 =$ _____ $+$ _____

$=$ _____

4 $9 \times 8 =$ _____

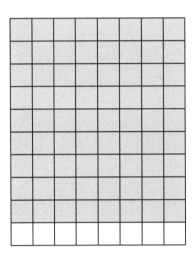

_____ $\times 8 =$ _____

_____ $\times 8 =$ _____

_____ $\times 8 =$ _____ $-$ _____

$=$ _____

5 $8 \times 8 =$ _____

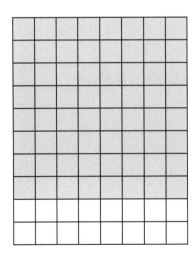

_____ $\times 8 =$ _____

_____ $\times 8 =$ _____

_____ $\times 8 =$ _____ $-$ _____

$=$ _____

Extra Practice and Homework
Multiplication Tables

Activity 4   Multiplying by 9

Find and circle the multiplication facts of 9 in the puzzle.
The multiplication facts (without operation signs) can be vertical,
horizontal, or diagonal.
An example has been done for you.

1

2	18	45	9	10	4	10	81
36	9	6	9	54	9	9	81
5	9	18	1	3	36	90	63
5	63	81	54	9	45	81	6
90	9	27	4	27	9	10	90
9	7	45	9	5	54	81	27
10	90	3	36	9	4	9	36
19	27	42	27	45	81	20	63

**Multiply. Use multiplication facts you know to find other
multiplication facts.**

2 $7 \times 9 =$ _____

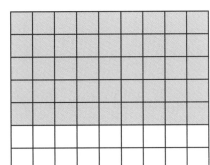

_____ $\times 9 =$ _____

_____ $\times 9 =$ _____

_____ $\times 9 =$ _____ $+$ _____

          $=$ _____

3 $9 \times 9 =$ _____

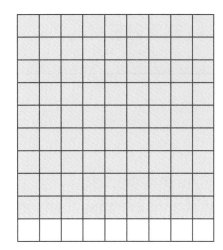

_____ $\times\ 9 =$ _____

_____ $\times\ 9 =$ _____

_____ $\times\ 9 =$ _____ $-$ _____

$=$ _____

4 $8 \times 9 =$ _____

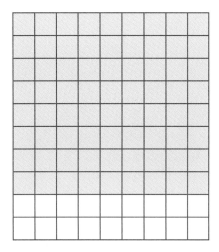

_____ $\times\ 9 =$ _____

_____ $\times\ 9 =$ _____

_____ $\times\ 9 =$ _____ $-$ _____

$=$ _____

5 $6 \times 9 =$ _____

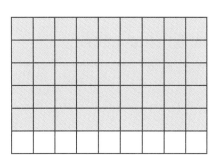

_____ $\times\ 9 =$ _____

_____ $\times\ 9 =$ _____

_____ $\times\ 9 =$ _____ $+$ _____

$=$ _____

Extra Practice and Homework
Multiplication Tables

Activity 5   Multiplying by 11

Find and circle the multiplication facts of 11 in the puzzle.
The multiplication facts (without operation signs) can be vertical,
horizontal, or diagonal.
An example has been done for you.

1

11	22	77	11	7	2	44	22
77	88	66	11	6	11	11	55
7	11	77	1	4	2	99	66
5	8	7	3	11	33	77	9
11	2	11	22	44	10	11	110
55	33	33	88	110	99	110	3
1	11	11	6	66	9	11	99
55	99	44	82	44	33	99	88

Solve. Show your work.

2   Hannah says that she can find the product of 11 and any 1-digit
number without having to write it down. How do you think this is
possible? Explain.

_____

_____

_____

Find each missing number. Use mathematical facts of 11 to help you.

3 Bella the bird only eats worms that carry numbers that are products of 11. Cross out the worms that Bella the bird does not eat.

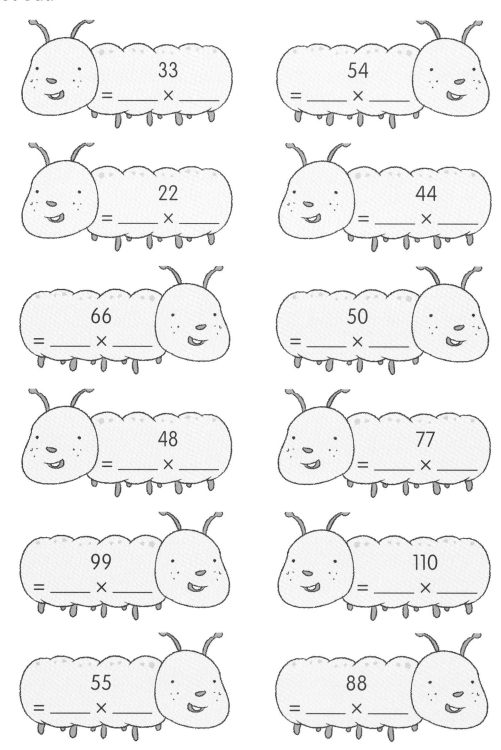

33 = _____ × _____

54 = _____ × _____

22 = _____ × _____

44 = _____ × _____

66 = _____ × _____

50 = _____ × _____

48 = _____ × _____

77 = _____ × _____

99 = _____ × _____

110 = _____ × _____

55 = _____ × _____

88 = _____ × _____

Chapter 4

Extra Practice and Homework
Multiplication Tables

Activity 6   Multiplying by 12

Find and circle the multiplication facts of 12 in the puzzle.
The multiplication facts (without operation signs) can be vertical,
horizontal, or diagonal.
An example has been done for you.

 1

10	2	12	108	10	120	96	5
5	12	60	12	5	4	8	12
1	24	120	6	12	72	12	60
60	4	12	48	60	10	96	9
84	12	7	48	3	12	36	12
72	48	9	12	108	120	5	108
3	12	36	60	84	12	7	84
108	36	45	72	60	108	35	192

Solve. Show your work.

2 James says that because 12 is in the multiplication table of 4,
any number in the multiplication table of 12 will also be in the
multiplication table of 4. Is James correct? Explain.

_____

_____

_____

Multiply and match. Use mathematical facts of 12 to help you.

Ms. Brown went fishing. She caught some fish. She kept them in different boxes. Find out which fish was stored in which box.

3

5 × 12 = _____ •

• 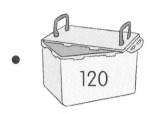 120

4

3 × 12 = _____ •

•  48

5

8 × 12 = _____ •

•  108

6

7 × 12 = _____ •

•  84

7

4 × 12 = _____ •

•  96

8

9 × 12 = _____ •

•  36

9

10 × 12 = _____ •

•  60

Chapter 4

Extra Practice and Homework
Multiplication Tables

Activity 7   Multiplication Patterns

Solve.

1   Skip count by 6. Shade the boxes with numbers found in the multiplication table of 6.

1	2	3	4	5	6	7	8	9	10
11	12	13	14	15	16	17	18	19	20
21	22	23	24	25	26	27	28	29	30
31	32	33	34	35	36	37	38	39	40
41	42	43	44	45	46	47	48	49	50
51	52	53	54	55	56	57	58	59	60
61	62	63	64	65	66	67	68	69	70
71	72	73	74	75	76	77	78	79	80
81	82	83	84	85	86	87	88	89	90
91	92	93	94	95	96	97	98	99	100

2   What do you notice about the numbers?

_____

_____

_____

3 Write down the ones digit of the next three numbers in the multiplication table of 6 after the last shaded box.

_____

4 Skip count by 7. Shade the boxes with numbers found in the multiplication table of 7.

1	2	3	4	5	6	7	8	9	10
11	12	13	14	15	16	17	18	19	20
21	22	23	24	25	26	27	28	29	30
31	32	33	34	35	36	37	38	39	40
41	42	43	44	45	46	47	48	49	50
51	52	53	54	55	56	57	58	59	60
61	62	63	64	65	66	67	68	69	70
71	72	73	74	75	76	77	78	79	80
81	82	83	84	85	86	87	88	89	90
91	92	93	94	95	96	97	98	99	100

5 What do you notice about the numbers?

_____

_____

_____

6 Write down the ones digit of the next three numbers in the multiplication table of 7 after the last shaded box.

_____

7 Skip count by 8. Shade the boxes with numbers found in the multiplication table of 8.

1	2	3	4	5	6	7	8	9	10
11	12	13	14	15	16	17	18	19	20
21	22	23	24	25	26	27	28	29	30
31	32	33	34	35	36	37	38	39	40
41	42	43	44	45	46	47	48	49	50
51	52	53	54	55	56	57	58	59	60
61	62	63	64	65	66	67	68	69	70
71	72	73	74	75	76	77	78	79	80
81	82	83	84	85	86	87	88	89	90
91	92	93	94	95	96	97	98	99	100

8 What do you notice about the numbers?

_____

_____

_____

9 Write down the ones digit of the next three numbers in the multiplication table of 8 after the last shaded box.

_____

10 Skip count by 9. Shade the boxes with numbers found in the multiplication table of 9.

1	2	3	4	5	6	7	8	9	10
11	12	13	14	15	16	17	18	19	20
21	22	23	24	25	26	27	28	29	30
31	32	33	34	35	36	37	38	39	40
41	42	43	44	45	46	47	48	49	50
51	52	53	54	55	56	57	58	59	60
61	62	63	64	65	66	67	68	69	70
71	72	73	74	75	76	77	78	79	80
81	82	83	84	85	86	87	88	89	90
91	92	93	94	95	96	97	98	99	100

11 What do you notice about the numbers?

_____

_____

_____

12 Write down the ones digit of the next three numbers in the multiplication table of 9 after the last shaded box.

_____

13 What is the relationship between the numbers in the multiplication tables of 3 and 9?

_____

_____

14 Skip count by 11. Shade the boxes with numbers found in the multiplication table of 11.

1	2	3	4	5	6	7	8	9	10
11	12	13	14	15	16	17	18	19	20
21	22	23	24	25	26	27	28	29	30
31	32	33	34	35	36	37	38	39	40
41	42	43	44	45	46	47	48	49	50
51	52	53	54	55	56	57	58	59	60
61	62	63	64	65	66	67	68	69	70
71	72	73	74	75	76	77	78	79	80
81	82	83	84	85	86	87	88	89	90
91	92	93	94	95	96	97	98	99	100
101	102	103	104	105	106	107	108	109	110

15 What do you notice about the numbers?

_____

_____

_____

16 Write down the ones digit of the next three numbers in the multiplication table of 11 after the last shaded box.

_____

17 Skip count by 12. Shade the boxes with numbers found in the multiplication table of 12.

1	2	3	4	5	6	7	8	9	10
11	12	13	14	15	16	17	18	19	20
21	22	23	24	25	26	27	28	29	30
31	32	33	34	35	36	37	38	39	40
41	42	43	44	45	46	47	48	49	50
51	52	53	54	55	56	57	58	59	60
61	62	63	64	65	66	67	68	69	70
71	72	73	74	75	76	77	78	79	80
81	82	83	84	85	86	87	88	89	90
91	92	93	94	95	96	97	98	99	100
101	102	103	104	105	106	107	108	109	110
111	112	113	114	115	116	117	118	119	120

18 What do you notice about the numbers?

_____

_____

_____

19 Write down the ones digit of the next three numbers in the multiplication table of 12 after the last shaded box.

_____

20 What is the relationship between the numbers in the multiplication tables of 3, 4, and 12?

_____

_____

Chapter 4

Extra Practice and Homework
Multiplication Tables

Activity 8   Dividing using Multiplication Facts

Find each missing number. Use related multiplication facts to help you.

1 Share 18 scones equally among 6 people. How many scones does each person receive?

_____ ÷ _____ = _____

| ☐ | × | 6 | = | 18 |

| 18 | ÷ | 6 | = | ☐ |

Each person receives _____ scones.

2 Diego puts 35 flowers equally in 7 vases. How many flowers are there in each vase?

_____ ÷ _____ = _____

| ☐ | × | 7 | = | ☐ |

| ☐ | ÷ | 7 | = | ☐ |

There are _____ flowers in each vase.

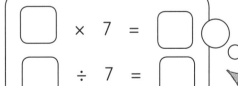

3 Mr. Cook sews a total of 72 buttons onto some dresses. He sews 8 buttons onto each dress. How many dresses are there?

_____ ÷ _____ = _____

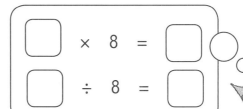

☐ × 8 = ☐

☐ ÷ 8 = ☐

There are _____ dresses.

4 Ms. Jones has 63 coins to share equally among some children. Each child receives 9 coins. How many children are there?

_____ ÷ _____ = _____

☐ × 9 = ☐

☐ ÷ 9 = ☐

There are _____ children.

© 2020 Marshall Cavendish Education Pte Ltd

Extra Practice and Homework Grade 3A

5 Ms. Clark shares 22 markers equally among 11 students. How many markers does each student receive?

_____ ÷ _____ = _____

☐ × 11 = 22

☐ ÷ 11 = ☐

Each student receives _____ markers.

6 Ms. Garcia shares 60 tennis balls equally among 12 students. How many tennis balls does each student receive?

_____ ÷ _____ = _____

☐ × 12 = 60

☐ ÷ 12 = ☐

Each student receives _____ tennis balls.

Find each missing number. Use mathematical facts to help you.

7 $8 \times 9 =$ _____

_____ $\div 9 =$ _____

$9 \times$ _____ $=$ _____

_____ $\div$ _____ $= 9$

8 $5 \times 11 =$ _____

_____ $\div 11 =$ _____

$11 \times$ _____ $=$ _____

_____ $\div$ _____ $= 11$

9 $2 \times 8 =$ _____

_____ $\div 8 =$ _____

$8 \times$ _____ $=$ _____

_____ $\div$ _____ $= 8$

10 _____ $\times 7 =$ _____

_____ $\div 7 =$ _____

$7 \times 4 =$ _____

_____ $\div$ _____ $= 7$

11 _____ $\times 12 =$ _____

_____ $\div 12 =$ _____

$12 \times 6 =$ _____

_____ $\div$ _____ $= 12$

12 _____ $\times 6 =$ _____

_____ $\div 6 =$ _____

$6 \times$ _____ $=$ _____

_____ $\div$ _____ $= 6$

Write two multiplication equations and the related division equations using the given numbers and operation signs.

13

| 7 | 42 | 6 | × | ÷ | = |

14

| 72 | × | ÷ | 9 | 8 | = |

15

| 90 | × | 9 | 10 | ÷ | = |

Solve. Show your work.

16 Sara has 24 hair clips. She wants to pack them equally into some gift bags. What are some possible ways that Sara can pack her hair clips? Explain how you would do it. Use drawings or words to help you.

17 Zane has 56 stickers. He wants to decorate each of his greeting cards with an equal number of stickers. What are some possible ways that Zane can decorate the greeting cards? Explain how you would do it. Use drawings or words to help you.

18 These are 72 desks. Ms. Cooper wants to arrange the desks equally in rows in a classroom. What are some possible ways that Ms. Cooper can arrange the desks in the classroom? Explain how you would do it. Use drawings or words to help you.

Mathematical Habit 2 **Use mathematical reasoning**

In this chapter, you have learned about multiplication tables. Look at the mathematical equation below.

$$6 \times 8 = 48$$

If the first number is reduced by half and the second number is doubled, what happens to the product? Explain.

MATH JOURNAL

Mathematical Habit 1 Perservere in solving problems

Mr. Green has altogether 100 dung beetles and spiders in his collection. The creatures have a total of 740 legs. How many dung beetles and spiders does Mr. Green have?

Dung beetles (6 legs)	Spiders (8 legs)	Total number of legs	Correct (✔) / Wrong (✗)

Guess and check your answer.

Mr. Green has _____ dung beetles and _____ spiders.

SCHOOL-to-HOME
CONNECTIONS

Chapter 5

Multiplication

Dear Family,

In this chapter, your child will learn to multiply up to 3-digit numbers by a 1-digit number. Skills your child will practice include:
- multiplying using models
- multiplying without regrouping
- multiplying with regrouping

Math Practice

There are numerous real-life opportunities for your child to multiply. At the end of this chapter, you may want to carry out these activities with your child. These activities will help your child practice multiplying numbers.

Activity 1

- At home or in a supermarket, look at a package of hot dog or hamburger buns.
- Ask your child to count the number of buns in the package.
- Then, ask your child to calculate how many buns there are in 9, 10, and 11 packages, if all the packages have the same number of buns.

Activity 2

- Egg cartons usually hold between 6 and 12 eggs. Have your child count the spaces in an egg carton that you have at home.
- Then, ask your child to calculate how many eggs there are in 5 egg cartons if all the cartons hold the same number of eggs.

Math Talk

Help your child understand the meaning of the word **product**, which is the answer to a multiplication problem.

Look at the following together and ask your child to find the product.
$5 \times 70 = ?$
The product of 5 and 70 is 350.

Encourage your child to write and solve a multiplication problem, naming the product.

BLANK

Name: _____ Date: _____

Chapter 5 Extra Practice and Homework
Multiplication

Activity 1 Multiplying Using Models

Use the array model to find each missing number.

1 16 × 8 = ?

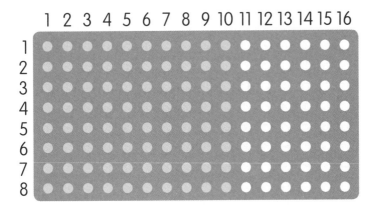

16 × 8 = (_____ × 8) + (_____ × 8)

= _____ + _____

= _____

2 15 × 6 = ?

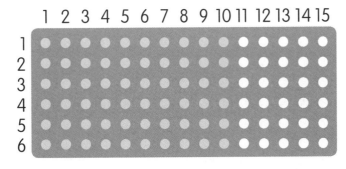

15 × 6 = (_____ × 6) + (_____ × 6)

= _____ + _____

= _____

© 2020 Marshall Cavendish Education Pte Ltd

Extra Practice and Homework Grade 3A

1 Multiplying Using Models

3 $13 \times 5 = ?$

$$13 \times 5 = (\underline{\hspace{1.5cm}} \times 5) + (\underline{\hspace{1.5cm}} \times 5)$$

$$= \underline{\hspace{1.5cm}} + \underline{\hspace{1.5cm}}$$

$$= \underline{\hspace{1.5cm}}$$

4 $15 \times 7 = ?$

$$15 \times 7 = (\underline{\hspace{1.5cm}} \times 7) + (\underline{\hspace{1.5cm}} \times 7)$$

$$= \underline{\hspace{1.5cm}} + \underline{\hspace{1.5cm}}$$

$$= \underline{\hspace{1.5cm}}$$

5 $14 \times 3 = ?$

$$14 \times 3 = (\underline{\hspace{1.5cm}} \times 3) + (\underline{\hspace{1.5cm}} \times 3)$$

$$= \underline{\hspace{1.5cm}} + \underline{\hspace{1.5cm}}$$

$$= \underline{\hspace{1.5cm}}$$

Use the area model to find each missing number.

6 $19 \times 7 = ?$

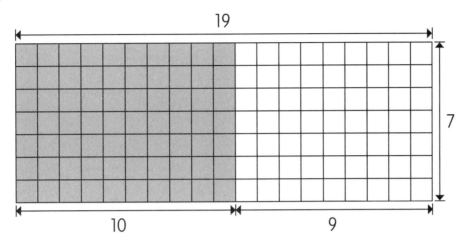

$19 \times 7 = (\underline{\hspace{1.5cm}} \times 7) + (\underline{\hspace{1.5cm}} \times 7)$

$= \underline{\hspace{1.5cm}} + \underline{\hspace{1.5cm}}$

$= \underline{\hspace{1.5cm}}$

7 $17 \times 5 = ?$

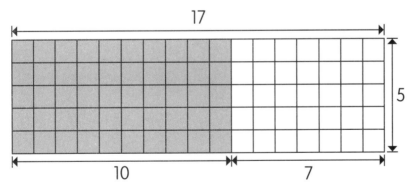

$17 \times 5 = (\underline{\hspace{1.5cm}} \times 5) + (\underline{\hspace{1.5cm}} \times 5)$

$= \underline{\hspace{1.5cm}} + \underline{\hspace{1.5cm}}$

$= \underline{\hspace{1.5cm}}$

8 18 × 4 = ?

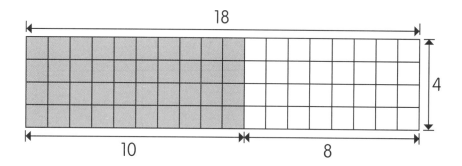

18 × 4 = (_____ × 4) + (_____ × 4)

= _____ + _____

= _____

9 16 × 9 = ?

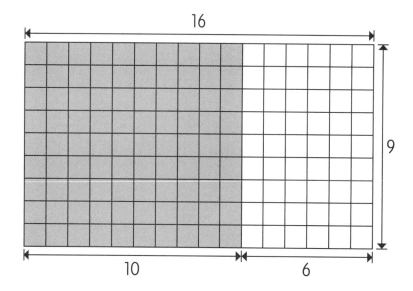

16 × 9 = (_____ × 9) + (_____ × 9)

= _____ + _____

= _____

10 41 × 5 = ?

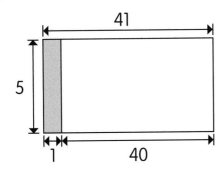

41 × 5 = (_____ × 5) + (_____ × 5)

= _____ + _____

= _____

11 38 × 9 = ?

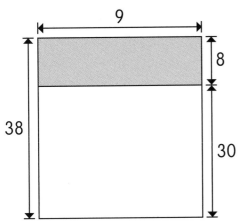

38 × 9 = (_____ × 9) + (_____ × 9)

= _____ + _____

= _____

12 36 × 7 = ?

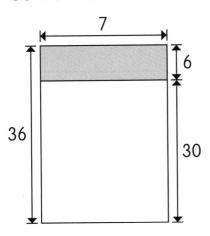

36 × 7 = (_____ × 7) + (_____ × 7)

= _____ + _____

= _____

13 153 × 4 = ?

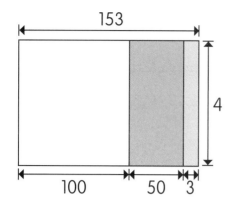

153 × 4

= (____ × 4) + (____ × 4) + (____ × 4)

= _____ + _____ + _____

= _____

Fill in each blank on the area model. Then, use the area model to multiply.

14 26 × 9 = ?

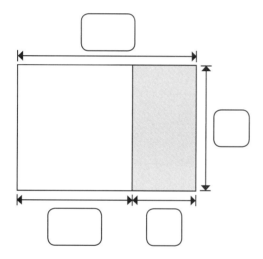

15 222 × 7 = ?

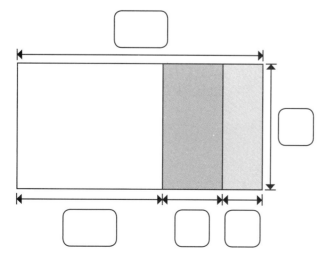

Extra Practice and Homework
Multiplication

Activity 2 Multiplying Without Regrouping

Find each missing number.

1 6×50

= $6 \times$ _____ tens

= _____ tens

= _____

2 4×300

= $4 \times$ _____ hundreds

= _____ hundreds

= _____

3 70×3

= _____ tens $\times 3$

= _____ tens

= _____

4 300×2

= _____ hundreds $\times 2$

= _____ hundreds

= _____

5

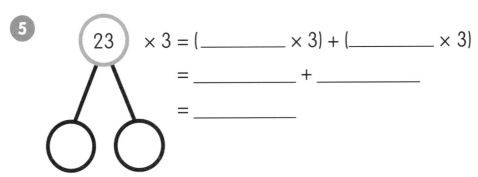

$23 \times 3 = ($ _____ $\times 3) + ($ _____ $\times 3)$

= _____ + _____

= _____

6

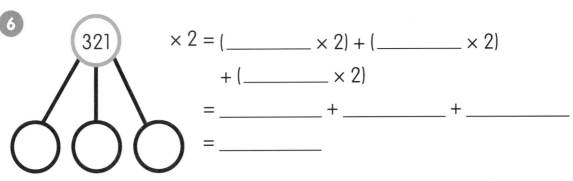

$321 \times 2 = ($ _____ $\times 2) + ($ _____ $\times 2)$

$+ ($ _____ $\times 2)$

= _____ + _____ + _____

= _____

Multiply.

7)
```
    2 1
  ×   5
```

8)
```
    3 0
  ×   8
```

9)
```
    4 2
  ×   3
```

10)
```
  1 1 0
  ×   6
```

11)
```
  1 1 1
  ×   5
```

12)
```
  1 3 2
  ×   3
```

13)
```
  2 1 2
  ×   4
```

14)
```
  1 0 1
  ×   4
```

15)
```
  3 1 2
  ×   2
```

16)
```
  1 1 2
  ×   3
```

Activity 3   Multiplying with Regrouping

Multiply and match.

1
$$
\begin{array}{r}
2\ 3 \\
\times\ \ \ 4 \\
\hline
\end{array}
$$
•

•  648

2
$$
\begin{array}{r}
7\ 9 \\
\times\ \ \ \ 4 \\
\hline
\end{array}
$$
•

• 565

3
$$
\begin{array}{r}
9\ 6 \\
\times\ \ \ 8 \\
\hline
\end{array}
$$
•

•  92

4
$$
\begin{array}{r}
1\ 1\ 3 \\
\times\ \ \ \ 5 \\
\hline
\end{array}
$$
•

•   654

5
$$
\begin{array}{r}
3\ 2\ 7 \\
\times\ \ \ \ 2 \\
\hline
\end{array}
$$
•

• 316

6
$$
\begin{array}{r}
1\ 0\ 8 \\
\times\ \ \ \ 6 \\
\hline
\end{array}
$$
•

•  768

7
```
    1 6 7
  ×     3
```
•   • ⟨3,024⟩

8
```
    1 3 9
  ×     7
```
•   • 1,782

9
```
    2 5 4
  ×     3
```
•   • 2,256

10
```
    2 3 4
  ×     4
```
•   • 1,896

11
```
    4 3 2
  ×     7
```
•   • 501

12
```
    3 7 6
  ×     6
```
•   • 936

13
```
    1 9 8
  ×     9
```
•   • 762

14
```
    2 3 7
  ×     8
```
•   • 973

© 2020 Marshall Cavendish Education Pte Ltd

Mathematical Habit 2 Use mathematical reasoning

You are given five number cards.

Form a multiplication equation using three number cards.
The product must be greater than 500.
Explain how you do this.

_____

_____

_____

_____

_____

Mathematical Habit 1 Persevere in solving problems

You are given three number cards.

a   Form a 2-digit number and a 1-digit number using the number cards. Then, write a multiplication equation that gives the greatest product.

_____

b   Form a 2-digit number and a 1-digit number using the number cards. Then, write a multiplication equation that gives the least product.

_____

SCHOOL-to-HOME
CONNECTIONS

Chapter 6

Using Bar Models:
The Four Operations

Dear Family,

In this chapter, your child will learn how to solve real-world problems involving the four operations (addition, subtraction, multiplication, and division). Skills your child will practice include:

- using models to solve real-world problems involving the four operations

Math Practice

Using bar models helps your child translate information from a real-world problem into its component parts. At the end of this chapter, you may want to carry out this activity with your child. This activity will help your child practice using bar models.

Activity

- Have your child state his or her age.
- Show the following bar model to your child. Ask your child: "How old is someone who is 8 times as old as you are?"

someone else's age
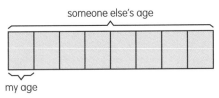
my age

- Next, show the following bar model to your child and ask: "How old would someone 24 years younger than that person (who is 8 times as old as you are) be?"

older person's age
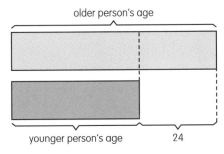
younger person's age   24

Math Talk

Help your child understand that he or she can use a **bar model** to represent the information in a real-world problem and to help him or her solve problems.

Ask your child to read the following real-world problem and then explain the bar model. You may need to remind your child that the word **twice** means two times.

There are 23 red pens. The number of blue pens is twice the number of red pens. How many blue pens are there?

23

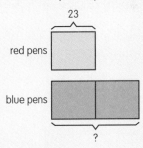
red pens

blue pens

?

$23 \times 2 = 46$
There are 46 blue pens.

BLANK

Chapter 6

Extra Practice and Homework
Using Bar Models: The Four Operations

Activity 1   Real-World Problems: Multiplication

Solve. Show your work. Use the bar model to help you.

1 Alex fills 9 pages with foreign stamps in an album. There are 7 stamps on each page. How many foreign stamps does Alex collect?

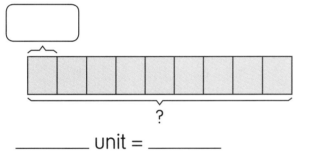

_____ unit = _____

_____ units = _____ × _____

= _____

Alex collects _____ foreign stamps.

2 I see 12 cats in a park. Each cat has the same number of legs. How many legs do the cats have in all?

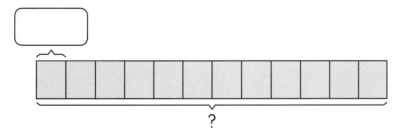

3 There are 5 exhibition rooms in a museum. There are 10 visitors in each room. How many visitors are there in all?

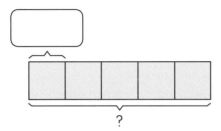

Solve. Show your work. Use the bar model to help you.

4 There are 8 levels in a parking garage. There are 11 cars parked on each level. How many cars are there in all in the parking garage?

Solve. Show your work. Use the bar model to help you.

5 Kylie bakes 6 cookies. She then bakes 3 times as many scones as cookies. How many cookies and scones does Kylie bake in all?

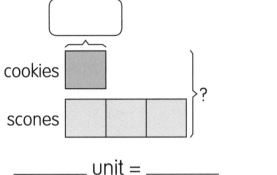

_____ unit = _____

_____ units = _____ × _____

= _____

Kylie bakes _____ cookies and scones in all.

6 There are 12 adults in a room. There are twice as many children as adults in the room. How many adults and children are there in all?

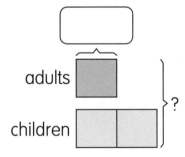

7 There are 11 coins in a bag. There are 6 times as many coins in a box as there are in the bag. How many coins are there in all?

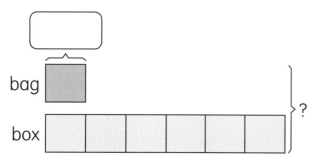

Solve. Show your work. Draw a bar model to help you.

8 Cole has 9 soft toys. He has 5 times as many action figures as soft toys. How many soft toys and action figures does Cole have in all?

Chapter 6

Extra Practice and Homework
Using Bar Models: The Four Operations

Activity 2   Real-World Problems: Division

Solve. Show your work. Use the bar model to help you.

1 Daniel has 90 red beans. He splits the red beans equally across 10 pots. How many red beans are there in each pot?

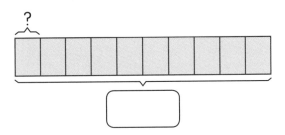

_____ units = _____

_____ unit = _____ ÷ _____

            = _____

There are _____ red beans in each pot.

2 72 students take part in a sports relay. They are divided equally into 8 groups. How many students are there in each group?

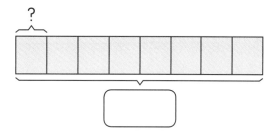

Solve. Show your work. Draw a bar model to help you.

3 Faith decorates 6 shirts with 42 beads. She uses an equal number of beads for each shirt. How many beads does she use to decorate each shirt?

4 Ali has 120 stickers and 12 cards. He wants to paste an equal number of stickers on each card. How many stickers does he paste on each card?

5 Ms. Turner had a total of 20 cups of tea in 5 days. She had an equal number of cups each day. How many cups did she have each day?

Solve. Show your work. Use the bar model to help you.

6 Mr. Brown gave 24 peaches to Carla and Caleb. Caleb received twice as many peaches as Carla. How many peaches did Carla receive?

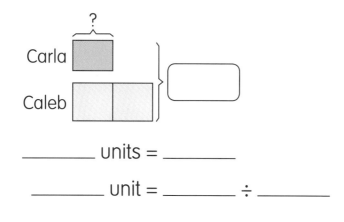

_____ units = _____

_____ unit = _____ ÷ _____

= _____

Carla received _____ peaches.

7 There are 36 cows on Ms. Lopez's farm. There are 6 times as many cows as sheep. How many sheep are there on Ms. Lopez's farm?

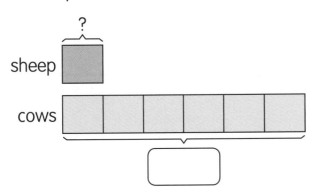

Solve. Show your work. Draw a bar model to help you.

8 Tyler has 48 fiction and non-fiction books in all. He has 3 times as many fiction books as non-fiction books. How many non-fiction books does Tyler have?

Chapter 6 Extra Practice and Homework
Using Bar Models: The Four Operations

Activity 3 Real-World Problems: Four Operations

Solve. Show your work. Use the bar models to help you.

1 There were 91 pens in a store. There were 28 fewer erasers than pens in the store. 9 students bought all the erasers. Each student bought an equal number of erasers.

a How many erasers were there in the store?

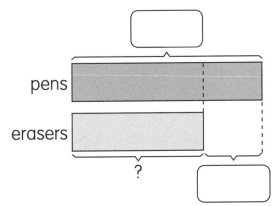

_____ ◯ _____ = _____

There were _____ erasers in the store.

b How many erasers did each student buy?

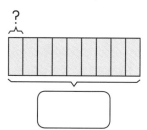

_____ ◯ _____ = _____

Each student bought _____ erasers.

Solve. Show your work. Draw bar models to help you.

2 Ms. Martin has 23 rings and 97 pairs of earrings. She places her jewelry equally into 10 boxes. How many pieces of jewelry are there in each box?

Solve. Show your work. Use the bar model to help you.

3 There are 108 children on a bus. The number of children is 12 times the number of adults on the bus.

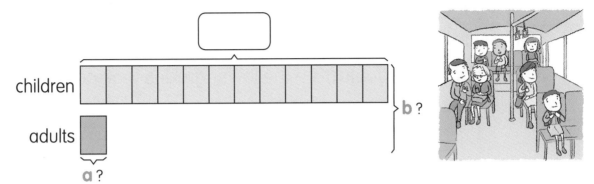

a How many adults are on the bus?

_____ units = _____

_____ unit = _____ ÷ _____

= _____

There are _____ adults on the bus.

b How many people are on the bus?

_____ ◯ _____ = _____

There are _____ people on the bus.

Solve. Show your work. Draw bar models to help you.

4 Some students took part in a school carnival game. The number of students from the upper grades was 3 times the number of students from the lower grades. The lower grade students were then divided equally into 6 groups of 10.

    a How many students from the lower grades took part in the game?

    b How many students took part in the game altogether?

Solve. Show your work. Use the bar models to help you.

5 Farmer Lee grows 75 stalks of wheat in a field. She grows 4 times as many stalks of corn as stalks of wheat.

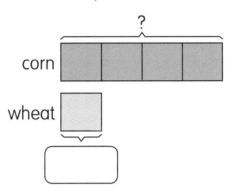

    a How many stalks of corn does Farmer Lee grow?

        ?

    corn

    wheat

_____ ◯ _____ = _____

    Farmer Lee grows _____ stalks of corn.

    b Farmer Lee harvests 124 stalks of corn. How many stalks of corn are left in the field?

        ?

_____ ◯ _____ = _____

    _____ stalks of corn are left in the field.

Solve. Show your work. Draw bar models to help you.

6 Bella makes 579 bracelets to sell. She wants to pack the bracelets into 12 boxes. 50 bracelets are packed into each of the first 11 boxes. How many bracelets will be packed into the last box?

Mathematical Habit 1 Persevere in solving problems

Number the steps for working out the real-world problem.

Real-world problem:

Lucas had twice as many stickers as Rachel. After Rachel bought another 50 stickers, Rachel had 3 times as many stickers as Lucas. How many stickers did Lucas have?

Number	Step
	Understand the problem.
	Lucas [bar model] Rachel [bar model with braces showing 50]
	Carry out the plan.
	Rachel bought another 50 stickers. We need to add these "50 stickers" to Rachel's model.
	Solve the problem by drawing bar models. Lucas [bar model] Rachel [bar model]
	Think of a plan to solve the problem.
	5 units = 50 1 unit = 50 ÷ 5 = 10 2 units = 10 × 2 = 20 Lucas had 20 stickers.

Mathematical Habit 4 Use mathematical models

Luis baked 51 strawberry, vanilla, and mango muffins. He baked 7 more strawberry muffins than mango muffins. He baked 4 fewer vanilla muffins than mango muffins. How many vanilla muffins did he bake?

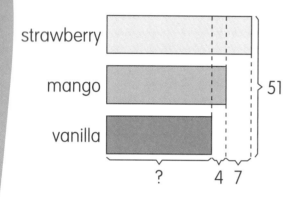